Fatto a Mano

Jerry Smaldone

Gerardo
10/15

Time is a Place

Edwin Forrest Ward

When all is said and done
then we shall stand as one
together

between the thousand pains
with death as a horse
and love at the reins

James Ryan Morris

For Michael Adamis

Richard Wilmarth and Lenny Chernilla

We live to embrace everything
and then one day we vanish
Lucien Blaga

Stata tenda la via

Known Associates
Jimi Bernath, Ed and Marcia Ward, Carson Reed,
RD Armstrong, Michael Annis, Ken Greenley, Karen
Armstrong, Jon Munson, Guillermo Lazo, Kathleen Cain,
Jared Smith, Lawrence Gladeview, Zack Kopp,
Claire Mearns and all at Turkey Buzzard Press.
Ken G, Alissa Smaldone and Mary Kay Smaldone for
technical advice. I owe you all more than you know.

Thanks to the Mercury Café, Ziggies, Glovinsky Gallery,
West Side Books, the Book Bar, all in Denver, Innisfree
Books in Boulder and Cannon Mine in Lafayette... and
to my angels and ancestors

Some of these poems appeared in Mad Blood,
Denver Crossroads, Lummox and Churn

contact jerry at   gsmal33@comcast.net

the author apologizes to all who consider poetry an art
Jonathan Williams

Fatto A Mano

Monday was Shkarol	2-3
Serena	4
Mount Olivet	5
45th and Navaho, 1928	6-7
45th and Navaho 1933	8-11
For Dad	12-3
Making Meatballs	14-5
We Sit on the Bench	16
Four Seasons	17
Michele di Fiero	18-27
Dream of Dad	28
Ci Vediamo Presto	29
Ti Benedic'	30
Clyde's 75th	31-3
Denver 1963	34-5
Northside Rules	36
Wingtips	37-9
Lakeside 1970	40
Mom's Angel	41-3
To Touch the Hand	44-5
Allora	46-7
Festa di Madonna	48-9
I love North Denver	50-2

Ascending Blindly

At Julie's B-day, Ziggie's	54
In This Room	55
I have so much	56
The Blind Singer	57
Follow your Bliss	58-9
As I Climb	60
I Don't Wanna Die	61
Ghosts	62-3
Poets	64
The Backyard	65
For Steve Wilson	66
I'm Gonna Live...Foreveh	67
For Mike Adams	68-9
Mailhandler's Lament	70-1
Lee the dogcatcher	72-3
Illumination-one	74-
Sacrament of Blood	76
Everywhere I go	77
Every Day Inside	78
This Bone Soreness	79
On The Road	80
White Buick Patrol	81
Awkward Gypsies	82
I Was Ashamed	83
Where my Heart Should Be	84
Thanksgiving	85
Our Place	86
Merry Xmas	87
Oh This Luck	88-9
Highways	90
Sector 7	91
for Og and Grog	92-3

Survivors at the Edge of Time

Belief	95
Heart, breaking	96
Day After Night	97
A duality, almost	98
Common Men	99
The Big Muddy	100
After the Storm	101
The Darkest Shadow	102-3
Having Given Up	104
House of Death	105
Mythological Scenario	106
The Prophet	107
He Awoke to a Dream	108-9
Finding the Hidden Door	110-11
Stalking Borderlands	112
What is Death	113
Where the Self	114
you, and god	115

Wound	116	Denver Again	148
Dislocation in the Market	117	.44 w/a Bullet	149-51
Media cosmology	118	The Noble Man	152-3
Pit Bulls at the Yard Sale	119	We Had it Easy	154-6
L'anima	120		
Inside every Atom	121		

Young Horses

Creative Destruction	122-3		
Ascoltaci	124-5	Name Names	158-9
The Sun	126-7	The Man in Black	160
The Lady	128-9	Do You Remember	161-3
Entanglement	130	Hold that piss	164-5
		Another Day	166-7

.44 with a bullet

Memory	132	Denver Exile	168
Leaving Work Early	133	Four for my son	
It's Hard	134	1-Leaders of the World	169
Gleason vs. Trujillo	135	2-He is Asleep	170
Life is a rude reminder	136	3-He is gone	171
Love has sunk her claws	137	4- I am here	172-3
One more time	138-9	Premature Mid-Life	174
Life Sucks	140	The last Jew	175
Ragged	142	Placebo Effect	176-7
For Dana	143	What the Mtn Tells	178
Each red petal	144	The Game	179
Cold macaroni	145		
When you opened	146	**Notes**	
Dark Wine	147		

Fatto a Mano

For Michael Smaldone

'Fatto giorno, siamo entrati in giuoco anche noi
Day breaks, and we too have joined the game...

Rocco Scotellaro

Before he died, 90 year old, still full of life, Ernest Borgnine was asked about his life and career. "When I was a boy, there was a guy on the corner selling hot chestnuts. God, they smelled good. I didn't have any money to buy them but I'd always walk by just to smell them. He had a sign on his cart that said, 'I'm not tryin' to set the world on fire, I'm just tryin' to keep my nuts warm.' And that's always been my my motto. It's how I lived my life."

Monday was Shkarol

Chicken soup with greens
Escarole, endive, diced carrot
Posteen and maybe, tiny meatballs

Tuesday, meekles and rice,
Thick or thin, a big cavaradd
Of lentils in a cunjamend,
A quick sauce of garlic, red pepper
A speck of tomato in oil, add water

Wednesday was savoy cabbage and
pigtails, maybe a neck bone, diced
potatoes in a cunjamend, add water,
Or kidneys and kidney beans
In a cunjamend

Thursday start the sauce.
Handful of dry basil, parsley,
Red pepper and garlic in oil
If they could afford it. Usually lard
Or salt pork. A spoon of cunzerve',
Brown the sausage or a rib, dash of wine
Add the tomatoes.

While it slowly bubbles, roll your dough
Out in thin sheets, cut the macs uneven
Ala straccinadd, no gitarra here.

Friday is pastafazool. Scraps of macaron'
With beans in a cunjamend'. Today we use
Elbow noodles. Dad likes big lima beans.

Saturday is bread day. Start the fire
In the forn', outdoor clay oven
Lined with brick, supported by timbers.
When the fire burns out, clear all
The ashes, take a wet mopeen,
An old flour sack, and wipe the steaming
Brick clean, set your loaves in with the paddle
And hang a wet mopeen over the door.

When the bread is done, bake rookle
For dinner. A round, porous loaf,
Thinner than bread, topped with tomato,
Grated romano, a sprinkle of parsley.

And finally, a thinner, crispy round
Of freetle, named for the fried leaf lard
From the pig's stomach, golden nuggets
Inserted into the loaf before baking,

So that when you bite into the hot loaf
Topped only with oil and romano
You crunch through the crispy freetle
And swear it's the best thing you've
Ever tasted.

Sunday, Thursday's sauce goes on the stove
Early, lettuce and tomatoes picked from
The garden, meatballs browned on the stove
For a snack and dropped gently into the sauce

Along with raw ones. The macs are rolled out,
Cut and boiled, tiny kitchen full of steam, as
Family files by, bread is broken, bottles of beer
And wine poured into little jam jars.

When a second heaping plate of spaghetti
Has been forced down, out comes the chicken,
Browned on the outside, tender inside,
Swimming in a sea of oil, onions, potatoes
And carrots and whatever else you want.
The salad follows for whoever can stomach it.

And Monday, Monday was shkarol.

A Cup of Coffee and Serena

He had to tell me the story more
than once before I got the point.

How his mother loved to sit
at the table with a cup of coffee.

How she turned 65, retired from the sewing
Job at Harmon Tailors just before they went
Belly up. How she found out, from nowhere,
That she would receive a small union pension.

How, with her daughter's meager earnings
she could afford the payments on the tiny,
plain house her children had built for her on
the lot paid for with the $800 she had saved
for you that you'd sent from overseas.

How she sat at the table in the little kitchen
Drinking coffee. Coffee was medicine,
Unaffordable as a child in Potenza, only
A spoonful at the farmaccia when sick.

Husband gone since 1926, children grown,
Family over on Sunday's for dinner,
A cup of coffee in a house of her own.

She sits and smiles, a slight smile,
Lifts the cup to her lips,
At peace, serena.

Mount Olivet

We forget so easily what does not haunt us.
       Aaron Abeyta

Walking past these graves
Another dead soul wandering in the shadows,
looking, looking for what, *il sangue miei morti,*
the blood of my dead? There in red granite is
another Jerry Smaldone, RIP, 1951, the year I was
born, and there, my grandfather, dead since 1926.

Familiar names of families, their entire
history resting in quiet memory, the key to
unlock these tombs, to explain these people,
is an unexplainable jump, or is it fall, into another

reality where these lives all happen at once,
Splashed across eternity, where the glories
and griefs, indiscretions and doubts are
illuminated for the soul to see.

From the grandest ornate marble
To the simplest weathered stone
Both hold lost wisdom and bleached bone,
The ground below wraps their secrets in a
blanket sewn of clearest light that reaches into
the earth and caresses what is here and yet gone.

To feel in your heavy feet their exhaustion,
to sing with the chorus of the dead,
Not in judgment because you're not
the Maestro but to be one with the
awakened that long to rise and disappear.

Pray, stop and pray, the dead need our
Prayers in their travels, to reach the visions
That will salve their souls, heal their wounds
Open them to the everlasting light and
The love that endures.

45th & Navaho, North Denver, 1928

They played in the swamp that ran from Pecos to Lipan, 46th to 48th and beyond the city limits, down the hill running into the Argo Brick tower, the Platte River, Globeville on the other side. It was their own wilderness, even the cactus had ripe plums to eat. They follow the goatherd as he pushes the goats home, stopping to cut long, green cattail spears and a young willow. A trickle of women, bundles of dandelions balanced on their heads, follows behind.

Home was on 45th, a tract of one acre plots. (He raises his eyes to mine, asks for a pencil and diagrams exactly where all dozen families lived and what their names were. It's been seventy-five years since he lived there.) The goatherd lives next door. He pushes the herd into his shed as the boys look through the window lined with hanging baskets. It is Easter time and orders are coming in for kid goats, caprett', tender from mother's milk, for the special meal.

He slips the cutidd from his sock, picks up a kid by the leg as it squeals like a baby, and with a deft move punctures its throat. Hot blood streams into a tin bucket. He'll use this to make sanguinadd, blood sausage. He hangs the kid up, makes a cut in the hoof and pokes the willow he shaved on the way home up the kid's leg. He replaces it with a hollow cattail and cheeks puffed, blows. The skin expands like a balloon, off the body. He slides his little knife up the soft skin and peels off the coat, guts it, takes the stomach and drops it in a basket.

He sits on a stool and milks its mother. He reaches for a handful of the stomach and drops it into the basket of milk. This is the starter, the quaglia. He reaches into another basket and takes out half-formed cheese, smooth and pliable. He shapes it into a horse, a rabbit, a lamb. When he sells these at the feasts children yell for him, "Cavacadd"!

He cleans the knife and starts to work the flat, green cattail reeds. He cuts and folds and layers, pulling up the edges, rolling the handle. (The boy in the window, now an old man, wonders if he could remember how to do it.) The goatherd finishes the green basket and hangs it next to dry ones.

He pulls the red kerchief out and wipes his brow. He wanly shakes at the flies. He dips a tin cup into the basket of warm milk and tops it with fresh, steaming blood. He drinks deeply, white and red dripping down his chin, clinging to his thick, droopy mustache.

He is not a happy man. He beats his son and this bothers the boy in the window. The goatherd cannot know, or does he, that this skill, passed from father to son for generations, is about to end.

45th & Navaho, North Denver 1933

He shivered in his blankets behind the cold stove, all her heat lost during the night. He had to pee but waited for first light to trek out to the privy, or the bahk-a-house, as they called it. For some reason, he had dreamt of his father after all these years, ice on his handlebar mustache, leading the horse and peddler's wagon back up Navaho, not really a street, deep puddles straddled by muddy hills.

He remembered his shining, black eyes, the scary stories he Told with his combas around a jug of wine as the boy had huddled safely behind this same stove. "Condi li vat!" they'd bellow, slamming the table. There was the tale of disappearing children, of the butcher walking past the policeman every day with his bag full of lamb's heads, and how one night the carabiniere hears a cry coming from the sack. "Whatta you got in there," he asks the butcher? "Lamb's heads, for my dinner," he replies. The word for lamb and child can be the same. Is he telling the truth? But he looks nervous and the officer pulls the bag open... only to gasp at the grisly sight of children's heads. "Condi li vat!" Or the heartbroken fellow who visits the cemetery every night and can be seen with his dead girlfriend sitting on his lap. Or how his own mother warned him about a certain man, and when he had answered the door that night there the man stood, eyes red and glistening and when he looked down he saw hooves instead of feet. His mother gasped and slammed the door behind him, took pictures of San Rocco, San Gerardo La Porto and San Michele Arcangelo and placed them on a chair facing the door, while she sprinkled the house with holy water. Anything could happen in old Potenza. "Condi li vat", he laid out his hands, count the facts.

Every day was a battle for Pa, to get the best produce, to maintain Your route, a fight for every inch, mostly against your own people, your competitors. Yet, Pa was home every night, not at the bar, helping his wife, unlike most of his friends. He thought of the little peace the man had known in his short life, the little bench he'd built in back, the boy sitting on his lap, wrapped in a strong arm, his small sisters safe and warm in the other. How he stared across the field of asparagus and pheasant tails to the purple mountains, a salve for his soul. Twenty five years of hard labor, of scrimping to get a small piece of land for himself, and now he was gone.

The boy crawled out of his covers and ambled to the outhouse, working out the kinks, trying to forget these last seven years. He was terribly alone and didn't know how to say it. Besides, everyone had their problems, why should they care?

He cuts dry cardboard to put in his shoes, feeds the chickens and gathers the few eggs, pumps water, pokes around the little barn. A broken leather strap lays in the matted hay, all that's left of the harness, the horse, the cow, the pig, the small crop. And soon the house would be gone, he'd heard his mother say. And where would they go then?

He sees cousin Packy, grinning in his off-centered way, coming down from his uncle's farm on Pecos. He considers walking to the end of the Argo street car line to pick up some snipes to smoke but it's too late. They walk down Navaho until the road dries out. He knows the names of every family in every house. He was born with a natural memory. They cross Columbus Park, hoping again to see a bootlegger's model T take the curve on two wheels, fleeing just ahead of the g-men, guns blazing.
Here, in the heat of summer the feast of our lady will be held. During the procession, the brass-buttoned band will play, fireworks will explode, floats overflowing with fresh flowers and angel-dressed children will parade and Mortadoot, the little hammer, will light his hot air balloon, fire glowing like a magic machine in the dusky sky. Of course, the fireworks boss is missing an arm. His mother always takes them to the Feast, but it gets tiring, walking and walking with no money to spend, while Ma fries sausage and peppers for the crowd, and he watches kids eat crispalettes, with their invisible *sapore del pianto*.

They cross 38th and stop at S.E.Cheverill drugstore, salivating at the sundae a cute schoolmate eats at the counter. They cross the street to avoid the knot of young men in front of the bug theater, ogling young women. They stare through the window at Levine's department store, at bikes and sleds and clothes they'll never have, move on past the tailor's, the barber, the macaroni factory to the aroma of bread baking in backyard ovens. Men are clustered in groups, talking politics and sports, women in long dresses push baby carriages and drag youngsters by the hand.

In the alley, there's a crap game and Felix is the lookout. "Hey, why-ole," he calls to Felix, all of ten, who gives him the wrist motion for, "What's up… where you headed?" They cross 36th and Sister-school hill, where kids will sled all winter, hoping no one gets hit by the occasional car, make the sign of the cross as they pass Mt. Carmel Church, glad that

Father J is nowhere to be seen. They walk by C's grocery to a roar of voices and see a door fly open to the backroom bar and poker table. Somebody beat the dealer, but that won't last long, Pa used to say. He remembers the rare pail of beer he carried home from the Pine Cone Inn and how Pa's dog, sad-eyed Mendoleek, would rest his big jaw on Pa's knee, eyeing the fresh brew. Mendoleek didn't last long after Pa died.

They cross 35th to the fog of beer and cigars leaking from the Sunset Inn and sauce bubbling at Little Pepina's, pass rows of cramped shotgun houses, keeping an eye out for any toughs who might be looking for trouble, hurry by the Irish church, the Mexican restaurant and reach the north end of the 20th street bridge. They stop and stare over the wide expanse of the Platte River bottoms, teeming with tenements, shacks and tracks and patches of garden. He usually steered wide of the hobo camps, even though his soft-hearted mother would cook them an egg for a bit of work. Rising like a kingdom on the other side was downtown Denver, exotic wonderland of commerce. He couldn't cross here without thinking of his first funeral as an 8-year old altar boy. The small casket was open and inside it the body was burned black. The boy wasn't the first to crawl under the viaduct in search of pigeon eggs to sell to fancy downtown restaurants, only to be electrocuted by the street car wires. In the fog of funeral incense, women in black screamed and tore at their hair. The casket is loaded in a wagon, pulled by black horses to the street car line and transported to Mount Olivet. Then he remembered how Pa's casket had been built in the front room and the front window removed to get it out of the house after the period of mourning.

But he liked the long, slow walk across the viaduct. When he was alone, he would stop and look down at the busy patchwork below him, the tall brick buildings to the south, Globeville to the east, the soft hills of the Northside dense with cave-like homes, and best of all, the majestic mountains to the West, towering over all. There was adventure there, gold and fishing and hunting, cowboys and maybe even Indians. And there was power in those mountains, power and peace.

They stepped off the bridge right into Chinatown. On Independence Day, his uncle would buy giant rockets here. Anything that could explode could be bought here for pennies. Pa had bought him firecrackers once. Men sat outside, jabbering in a language full of mystery. He listened, trying to decipher what they might be saying. The strange smells of a foreign land struck him and he looked up at skinned geese and ducks and little pigs hanging in a window.

They cross the street to the fruit market. Here, the crates of grapes are stacked two men high on the sidewalk and he can hear the Italians dickering for a good price. Inside the doors are fruits and vegetables and across the street cabbages for the railroad being delivered by Italian and Japanese farmers. But it's vendemmia, grape harvest time and the anticipation of that first wine makes his mouth water. He remembers a barefoot boy, crushing grapes in the big wooden tub along with Pa in his special white boots. Next week, he'd be helping his uncles and cousins loads crates of their own.

They reach the 20th Street bath house and he and Packy have decided they need a shower, being almost grown men of 14. He was amazed how clean you could feel, as if every dirty corner had been rinsed in a rushing mountain stream, as if everything wrong was washed away.

They arrive at their destination, Curtis Street, home of endless arcades, theaters, barbershops and bars and places no boy should be. It was fun just being here. After a while, Packy gives him a nickel from his dad, Zi Gaet, and they enter the Casbah Theater and watch a triple feature while nibbling on raisins stolen from the cellar.
The finale is "Tong Wars", and when they exit the movie house into the dark night and enter dusky, deserted Chinatown, they hurry past the black alleys and shuttered storefronts, afraid they might be kidnapped into who knows what kind of evil.

Back on the bridge, they relax. It's easy to be brave now. He sees a dime in the gutter. Yeah! This is their lucky day. They stop at the first creamery they see and buy two milk nickels. Ice cream covered in thick chocolate. Does that hit the spot.

Back on dark, muddy Navaho, He's glad Packy's beside him. The night time noises don't seem so scary and he walks, not runs all the way home, trees hissing loudly under the autumn moon.

For Dad

Time is a metaphor for change

Armies of shadow beings
Cast our every move in
This arc of ages, where

The 90 year old remembers
Those who would be 150 today

And back and back, where the loss
Cannot recall itself, only you
Talking to the end of youth,

Talking to those you never knew,
To those who've passed into
The long silence.

This struggle of la vecchiaia, the old,
to just be, to breathe, to pray for patience,
for guidance, for the strength to bless your
unsure, hollow steps as you walk toward the end.
Pazienz'…. patience…
……………………………………………………
If you want to see him on Sunday afternoon
It's best to go to Mt. Olivet and stand before
The cold stone crypt in the shadowed hall,
Third one up, over your head.

This is where the chill wind always blows
Where he sits on the bench and talks to her,
Tells her what's doing, apologizes again
For his lack of attention.

"All your mother wanted was a little love…..
And none of us could give it to her."

Words, just words, so tired of words,
The echo of their reprimand in the face
of a complicated reality.

I want to bite the sizzle in the electric air
And burn every heartache I've ever had
In a fireball of golden love.
....

The old get older, each day another step
Along a rocky, climbing path, a rough balance
Before the last flight to freedom.

Behind his house, hollyhock grows among
The purslane and puncture vine, seed carried
By a tiny bird.

There is endive in patches, all the endive you
Can eat, under the privet, pushing out weeds,
Parsley enough for an army of rabbits.
"Soup, Uncle Joe used to make parsley soup.
You want some shkarol?"

He wonders where the rhubarb and lilacs
Have gone that once graced all these alleys.
Tomatoes lay tangled in emerald vines
Poking from overworked, black earth,
Sweet, hidden jewels.

A tossed peach pit sprouts into a slender wand,
Swells to a golden shade of overflowing fruit.
"I'm lucky with peach pits."
It's an accidental life of enough.

When you're 91, it's good to be
Out in the yard all day,
Sweating in the sun.

This is living, a cold beer in the shade,
A ball game waiting on TV.
"Where ya been, stranger," he says,
"you ain't been around all week."

Making Meatballs with Dad

We're watching the World Cup where it's 5-0, Germany.
The local fans look shell-shocked, suicidal. They send in
Two substitutes and brother says, It could be the greatest
Comeback in Brazil history. Yeah, replies Dad, it'll take
about five dead Germans layin' on the field.

You wanna help me make meatballs, he asks. It'll be
fisaree. Get a glass of wine and put on some music. You
want some Dino, I ask? No, he says without looking up,
Mills Brothers. The one with You Only Hurt the One You
Love. It makes me think of your mother.

Get out the big pot, the frying pan, get the ratacadd, it's
Hanging on the wall, and grate some cheese, he says.
You can clean up. I've found over the years that it helps
to clean you as you go. Well put. Get out a bowl from
down there, some tomatoes, and the hamburger.

He dumps the hamburger in a bowl, adds a dash of parsley,
basil, the garlic I've pressed not smashed, according to his
directions, the Romano I've grated, a handful of crushed
saltines, a couple eggs and mashes it together. You don't
use bread crumbs, I ask gingerly? Some people use
breadcrumbs, he says. He pores a dab of olive oil in the
pan and turns on the stove while I open cans of paste and
sauce and wipe the counter. Is that music on, I can't hear it,
he says, I don't know why I like the Mills Brothers.

We never used olive oil when I was a kid, he says. Couldn't
afford it. Or coria. Coria, you know what that is, don't cha?
That's the skin off the pig. We used lard. And lemme tell ya,
pal, lard makes a great sauce. No doubt, I think, how about
bacon grease?

Get me the ice cream scooper out of the second drawer. He
scoops a lump of hamburger out and fills a cookie sheet.
Then he picks a lump and one by one, rolls them in his hand.
Here, you do it. Not too hard, he says, just enough. As I roll,
he drops them in the pan. Don't let 'em cook too long, just a
little. The sauce'll cook 'em. Gimme the cunserv', he says and
I hand him the paste. He scoops it into the pot to brown,

adds garlic, dry basil and parsley. Not all the garlic, he says, save some for later. Get me the chitazell. I get the red pepper and shake.

He waits, adds the sauce, brings it to a boil and tells me to drop in the meatballs. Easy, he says, don't break 'em. Aunt Rose taught Mary Kay and she used chopped tomatoes, I say. Your aunt was a great cook but I don't like it chunky, he replies. I like it smooth. He turns the heat to simmer and says, and when you stir it, go easy, as Up the Lazy River comes on. Always easy. Remember, you're retired now. You should be getting' up at ten o'clock.

You wanna stay for dinner? Yer brother 'n me'll have it tonight and in a couple three days it'll be sabreet. Oh, you guys eat good, I say.

We cook... ran-jah, he blurts, a mess, it's a jin-yahd, he shrugs and makes a face, a process in the making. But between me and your brother, we do alright.

Yeah, yeah, he's ninety-five, he can still stand at the stove, he's doin' alright.

We sit on the bench
Before the cold crypt
And chant the rosary.

Dad tells us to say
Our silent goodbyes
And after a long pause

We raise our heads
When suddenly the voice
Of a songbird bursts forth

As if from the walls of stone
One, two, three gorgeous
echoed blooms of sound,
one for each of us.

We look at each other
as Mom sweeps over us
in golden light,

warm and forgiving,
back to the stars, whispering
I love you, too.

....

Dressed in black
The band waits
For the procession
To catch them

In midbreath
And slowly choke
Their hollow laughter.

And the muted drum
And cadenced horns
Lead the corpse
Into the waiting.

Four Seasons

*...there are seasons enough for everything infinite
to reverse again and sweep us up into its season.*
    Jared Smith, Looking into the Machinery

Ah, the destruction of youth, the demise of passion,
You, a mirage that fades each time I reach, each
Drink, each smoke, each disappointment, another
nail in the tin cameo that holds my heart in place.

We will go on, one of us real, one an illusion that
makes the passage of time, makes these words
bearable.

Surrounded by old photos of her, you sit back
And tell her your problems, raise issues
To make sure you both agree.

Part of you has died with her, part of you has changed
and that is not allowed if you are an old man. It's a
young man's world when the past flicks its ciggies
at your memories and mirrors can only sneer.

You apologize to her again, tears staining the vision
once guiltless and clear. Nothing can change the past.
(Nothing can change the past, it's over and best left.)

Dancing to Glenn Miller, one long lush clarinet ride
across the golden floor, holding this petite bundle of
contradictions you cannot live without, knowing how
hard it will be, and you a young dope and still wanting

her, the brake to your motion, the rocket that flies
from your grasp. You sit in the dusk of the old living
room on the wedding furniture bought with the money
she had saved from her job, you sit, numbstruck, and
feel her, feel her, more than when she was alive.

Michele di Fiero

It's always hot the first Sunday of August at the park. We're here for our family picnic. We've had our chiachierone and are ready to eat, all hundred and some of us. But first, there is the prayer. The old guy slowly rises and the crowd gathers round. "Madone, he mumbles, look at this cumaddia."
This part, one he never wanted, never imagined, gets harder every year. He's the old one, the last one alive from his generation. We make the sign of the cross and there is complete silence.

" We're all here, he says, because we love each other. Because we're still a family. Because we still want to be together….. well, most of us. The crowd murmurs in laughter. "Because we want our children to know they have somewhere to go when the chips are down. He encourages them to get to know one another, for that's the first step in relying on each other. He tells them to never, ever forget the sacrifice their grand-parents made, their parents made, tells of the hardships, all done for us, not for our comfort but for our success, our happiness in this new world. He tells them why America is the greatest country that has ever existed. There has never been a place this free. Never a place with this opportunity.

He asks them to pray for those departed, to pray more when we have problems. He tells them to be careful not to get too caught up in the world, in the good things, because God doesn't care about the good things. He only cares about how you lived, how you treated others, were you fair, were you honest, did you love your family. Don't forget, your first obligation is to your family…
not to yourself, to your children, not yourself.
Don't worry about a perfect life, he says, nothing's perfect. And don't kid yourself, the blueprint is laid out before you're born. There's nothin' you can do about it. Even the mistakes. Remember, you always want to make life easier. And the way to do that is to be nice and sweet and humble. All the things I'm not." More laughter.

His old bent body droops and he stops and a few young ones wonder if it's over. But the older ones know. He's thinking now of his own life. This you don't see everyday.

He tries to raise his arthritic head, he only knows people
by their shoes, he says. "I want you to know how much I love
you. All of you. The greatest joy I have... is sharing my life with
you. And I want you to know that I mean it, it's not bullshit,
it would be phony if I said that to the people I love."

My eyes get wet and I'm not the only one. His words are not just
an inspiration but an oath. Never forget. He is the keeper of the
names, from babies to the long since gone, the dates, the history.
He is our link to the past, he cares more about this family than
anyone here, and he knows it. He refuses to let this family die.

"Jer, get me a beer. Ohh, I don't know when to shut up."
Whhatta ya mean, I say, you were great. "I want these people to
know, he says, you can't be ...mangia la doyn-ya, wanting too much.
There's only one law, you have to get in line with God's will and
forget your own." Yes, and he knows it's the only way to meet death,
to accept it calmly without being callous or hard or afraid. And this
belief that life goes on, is eternal, that the real you lives on.

Then he sees a little girl looking at him and smiling and he pokes me,
"Hey, go get that little girl there, yeah, her, I think she wants to talk
to me." And I ask her if she wants to talk to Uncle Mike, her great-
great uncle, and she nods and says, Yes, but I don't think he'd want
to talk to me. And I laugh and say, Oh yeaaah, he WANTS to talk to
you. And while I'm struck by how we let the miracle of life pass us
by every day, for the next half hour, in the shade of the big
cottonwood, while others wait their turn, they have a lively discussion.
....
Lemme tell you somethin', he says. Dead people are forgotten.
La Bon'Am. If you don't pray for the dead, who will? My brother
drives him to each grave, takes him on the tour. He can't get out
of the car anymore, can't even reach Mama's crypt on the second
floor. He sits and prays that they're not forgotten. I think of how
little I know of these people, some dead a hundred years. I think
of an old familiar woman we saw in church. Who's that, I whispered.
I gotta find out before she dies, he replies. Grave after grave from
1918, the great epidemic. The young couple who were married and
died soon after, days apart, headstones next to each other.

Born at home with no birth certificate, his stories curl around the
edges of what is left. I'll be here someday, he says, si Di vol, God
willing. He tells tales of the names on the graves as we slowly cruise
through Mt. Olivet, graves he used to care for, plant and water

flowers, fix the stones. Now all he can do is pray. There's more dagos here than in North Denver, he says... and they're quieter, too.

....

"Where you goin', sit down." It seemed I always had my hand on the door knob after a long visit, when he would suddenly come alive, not wanting the company to go, and begin a complex tale that covered years, generations, until I relented, let go the knob, finally sat back down. Of fifteen cent haircuts at Sunset Barbers on Curtis St., ten chairs, how Camels cost a dime but you could get a pack of Fatimas for a nickel, two donuts for a nickel, but who had a nickel. How tomatoes were a dollar a bushel, now they're a dollar apiece, fer cryin' out loud, how a pair of Thom McCann's cost two bucks, and they were good shoes! How the pig farmers roamed the alleys, picking up slop buckets. I remember, he says, when guys started makin' twenty-five dollars a week, that was big money! He really had cardboard in his winter shoes to cover the holes. His first day at the new school, he wore a gas station shirt with the patch removed, dark green on light green.

But, this leads to all the ways he's lost out, screwed up, never got ahead, took the wrong turn in life, ignored the signs, and he starts in, cursing our bad luck, when luck has little to do with it. He denigrates every cha-trool he's ever known, even the famous high school coach he hated with a "purple passion". He pushes the back of his hand from under chin, yells "Coo-pat. That's what we got." He taught us to be responsible but the hand of fate is everywhere, ready to strike down the loftiest ambitions. Old age is made for regrets.

....

He talks about the Navy, the South Pacific, WW II. How they screwed the hinges off the mess door, leaving the lock on, to get at the grub, day after day. How meatless for weeks, they traded for half a mutton in Australia, but the boiled meat smelled so bad they dumped it overboard, yet it floated in their wake for a week, even the fish wouldn't eat it. "We still couldn't get rid of it!" Liberty stories, training stories, walking down 42nd St. in New York and seeing a long line of kids and asking What's the big deal? Why, it's Frank, Frank's here. Frank who, he asks? And with nothing better to do, he catches an early glimpse of ol' Blue Eyes in 1942. How the first thing you did when you got out of boot camp was get some "tailor-mades."

He says the most beautiful thing he ever saw was Bora Bora, his tiny 19' wide LCI 362 slicing through the Pacific, swallowed up and down by these giant waves for weeks and that bunch of seasick teenage sailors hitting the coral reef with thousands of colored fish and the blue, blue water and the two green mountains like emeralds poking out of the sea. His eyes had a far off look and I'd never heard him so poetic. How the natives in nothing but grass skirts paddled out in their outriggers to trade beads for soap and other goodies. "Palmolive, they'd only take Palmolive. Nothin' there but a radio shack and a French priest. He was happy 'cuz we'd go to his little church and donate.

We slept on the beach and watched the natives
drink home made beer and eat roasted pig. These little pigs were everywhere. Old Louie Zak from Buffalo went native. Took off into the jungle and didn't come back for weeks. We had to find him. It was paradise, pal. Now the jet set moved in and the guys are washin' dishes and the women are makin' beds. Civilization ain't worth a shit. Civilized people aren't good people." He points his finger like he always does for emphasis.

I think of my uncles saying the only bad things about the old days were the outhouses and flies. For that, you traded freedom, real freedom. "The beauty part of it was that you could do most anything, if you could get away with it," he says.

He tells you how he lost his roll on the last ship home, $1800, a lot of dough in 1945, the game was rigged but he played anyway, he blamed that damn Frenchman. Drank his way back to Denver on the train with generous discharges, got out at Union Station and asked the cabby if three bucks would get him to 41st and Shoshone, his sister's house. He came back just like he'd left, broke, and that night he was back tending bar, doing what he hated.

....

He talked about the stranger who bought them winter coats, picking up scrap coal behind the trains, freezing while you waited for the money to buy coal, watching the G-men raid an old abandoned house, pulled out, musta been a hundred barrels of booze, busted 'em up, you could smell that whiskey for weeks but it was a bonanza for me, I took all those staves home, easy to split for firewood." He tells me how to make sotapere', second wine, add the sugar and water to the stems, the rrrahp, all the crap that floated to the top, turning the car-nid to tap the barrel.

His first car is a '24 Chevy, or was it a '27 , wood wheels, then a '30 Model A, it was a chin-jone, a wreck. That last model T in '27 or '28 was a hand crank. You had had to set the spark, not too high, there were four coils and when you turned that crank, if you were smart, you moved your thumb or it could break it. If you jacked up the back it was easier to start because there was no friction on the pistons. And the accelerator was a handle on the column. The '29 had a big windshield but wasn't too comfortable, I'll tell you right now. Chrysler was a big innovator, pumped gas right to the carb and had the first heaters.

....

He is loud now but shy back then, in charge of a bar at age 16. The men would come straight up from Argo Brick 'cuz 41st ran right through and do their beer and shot. "You see a lot of strange things standing behind a bar". When we got kicked out of our rental and couldn't get a loan, it was the bar owner, his brother-in-law, Uncle Frank who loaned him ten grand to buy a lot and build his own house. He still remembers the envelope with ten thousand dollar bills. And he paid him back the same way, with ten thousand dollar bills.

There was the hobo village just east of Argo, trains with hundreds of people hanging off them moving through what is now the Mousetrap at I-70 and I-25. Where were they going, he wondered?
How the bums came by on Sundays when Ma was home, she'd always feed them something for a little useless work.

He talks about Merchant Park, the Post Tournament, where the Cuban All-Stars played the White Elephants from Five Points, and Halliburton Cement played the bearded House of David. Teams from Arkansas, Oklahoma, M&O cigars from Kansas City, the big ball diamond and scoreboard on the side of the Denver Post building during the World Series, how the big crowd waited in the street to see the figures moved around the bases as the announcer called the game live.

Women were dames, dolls, and if they pushed him, broads. Being with him is like being in a black and white movie from the '30's.

He was a quiet kid who came from the edge of town, didn't have buddies around church. As an altar boy, the clique picked on him. One day, a kid grabs his hat and Dad goes after him. But the head altar boy, an older guy named Tony Politano, gets control and sets up a fight in the sacristy. Dad knocks the kid into a priest's locker and cuts him up good. And walking to Regis he'd get hassled by a crowd every day. One older guy says, if I get these guys to go one on one, are you in? Sure, he says. He bloodies the first kid up good and nobody else wants a piece.

....

Just about the time I got tired of going around his house to the unlocked back door, his numerous falls led to a wheelchair, then a walker and he moved to the end of the couch, overlooking the big picture window in the front room. He sits in a pile of papers, boosted by pillows. If he knows I'm coming, he unlocks the door. And I made a key. "Ghiama le fricatt, why-ole." My legs are screwed, kid. I remember the old car breaking down a few blocks from home. I'm 16, 17, hot dog athlete. We're walking, when he says, you wanna run. Sure, I think, I hope the old fart can keep up. But he starts striding out, faster and faster, me trying to stay even, we get to our corner and he turns it on. It wasn't even close.

"Chioda la port, shut the door." This one who was always hot, is finally cold, wearing his beat up jacket and coopaleen all day. No more driving, though he pretends he still can, just a little mobility is all he wants, this guy who loved to roll some wreck through the mountains just to get away. We called it fishing.

I hand him the fat wad of junk mail and ask him what's up. "Ay, when you're 95, all you can do is wait for somebody to show up. I go from this chair to that chair to this chair. Okay, he says, looking at his trove of junk mail. "Here's what you're gonna do for me today. Write these people and tell them to quit sending me t-shirts. And no more calendars. And make sure you drop off these letters for me." For the hell of it, I count them. Eighteen. 18 checks to 18 charities. He gives out money every week.
He hands me a letter. "Do you know these old Indians live out in the

boonies with no heat? In the middle of winter? He looks at another. Ay, you know I got a soft spot for Indian kids."

....

The older he gets, the more his Potenzaze dago lingo returns. Not just ten ways to call you dummy. Funny how the mind works. You look good today, I tell him. He gives me a sharp sideways glance. "Dummy up, he says, I'm not buying that crap. If you live long enough, you'll look pretty ugly. Whatta you expect? Oggia fatta faccia. I got old."

I pick something off his chin. "Get me a salvieth. And get yourself a coke. I'm okay, I say, I'm not thirsty. " Don't gimme that crap, you're la scopa dintre la port. This is one of the few phrases I know. The broom behind the door. The too quiet one. "Ah, nobody in this family is sfachadd." What's sfachadd? His shoulders droop dramatically and he smacks his forehead. "Don't choo know ANY Italian, he bellows as I laugh. You know, bold. You gotta fa la vach, show your face. So, how's the house coming?" I never should have mentioned it. "Ah, he shakes his head in fake disgust, cry pu scry!" He's implying I'm putting things off until...never.

"Getta load o' this, he says, did you know there's a thousand shapes of macaroni?" I thought it was maybe 150.
"The beauty part of it is, they got a shape for everything." This is what he learns from the cooking shows, and a dozen ways to cook pork chops. He's fascinated by cooking meat, probably because he didn't grow up eating it and never could cook it. "It's just not sa-breet, like your mother's,". Another way he misses her. Along with the household improvements she forced on him, like the rail he leans on as he climbs the outside stairs. "If your mother hadn't done this when I told her not to, I couldn't leave this house."

His swollen legs and broken knees are wrapped in gauze leggings that show from under the tattered sweatpants we've tried to get him to give up. I squeeze them to test the fluid. "My knees are shot but my mouth's still running. He stares at me. You okay?" He cares more about me than himself. The usual, I say, mezzomort. "Si Fatta vecchia! You look like an old man."

"Hey, get me a mezza tazza caffe." I slowly figure that out and pour a half cup from the coffeemaker which has no off switch. Neither does his talk. " You need to have some fun, he says, fa li fisareel! Fatta la spez, spend some money! You know, he says, giving me a look, you're kind of a strange Italian!" Really? "Here, setta la zang," he says, patting the couch. "See, even though I'm cranky, I'm not miserable." He cracks me up.

Did you eat today, I ask? "Nah, there's only meat here, he says, I can't eat meat anymore. I'm not a carnaroot anymore. But find me a cookie. I'm turning into a lu-cooch." He gobbles a couple. Sachiadd? I ask, throwing one back at him. Satisfied? Now I get it. This is a test, a game. Where's that soup you had? "Lo mangiat' tutt. I ate it all." That's good. When old people quit eating, it's all over.

We talk about the club. " I don't see too many nutcrackers in there, he says… some nuts, maybe. People are just who they are. If you don't expect miracles from 'em, you'll never be disappointed."

He picks up another letter. "Lemme tell ya, pal, when I was growing up, it was the ooold tough game. If you didn't work, you starved. If you didn't have any money, you starved. I always walked the curb. "Yeah, there was people going through the dumpsters at the packing plants downtown, not bums, regular people. When the Post had their jackrabbit hunt and giveaway, you shoulda seen the crowd. They blocked off 15th and 16th on Champa. That pile of rabbits seemed big as a house. And there was a limit of two. You only got two."

His eyes are alight but I realize that as he's gotten older the stories have gotten shorter, less detailed. He takes ten steps and he's out of breath. His head drops and for a second he rests.

"Do you ever say hello to your mother?" I'm baffled. What? "Right behind you." I turn to the side table by the door where her shrine rests, pictures, rosaries, holy cards, birthday cards, holy water, candles, mementos. I think of how he misses her. How he beats himself up for being so stubborn, inattentive. A typical husband. "I talk to her every day," he says. I think of the old days when it was funeral after funeral. Their new hobby, he said. Date night, she called it.
Yeah, yer mother and me, they thought we were yelling at each other, but we were just com-mu-ni-ca-ting." When I complain, he says, "Hey, there's very few compatible marriages." Words of wisdom. I think of them dancing to Perry Como at Elitch's, how they knew they'd

marry as soon as they met, at the way they depended on each other so much without even knowing it. So, I ask, how did you ask Mom to marry you. "I don't think I really did," he says, in that bewildered but honest way of his.

....

Every day he begins or ends a sentence with, "If I'm still around… as in, "If I'm still around next summer, we're gonna do ….."", the plans have become very short-term, for fixing things, for travelling, unable to repair, to work around the house, life has become so different with no spouse, no one to care for, no sick and broken relatives and neighbors, no helping out at the church, the bazaar, no daily mass, no coffee with friends.

We were sitting there, one day long ago, as he went on as he always did, about how the world had gone to hell, the neighborhood, where you giggle inside until his utterly thorough negativity drowns out all feeling, how nobody cares about the family anymore when it used to be all you had, and my sister tries to gently, or not, bring him back to the glories of life we take for granted. And he relaxes and agrees to try, but it's too easy to tease him about family.

And so I ask, if your fifth cousin or some coomba you haven't seen in twenty years breaks down in Utah, you go help him…?, he slams his hand down, voice booming, "Damn right, … You drop everything and you go!"
On the spot? And he gives me a wounded look, "You just don't get it, do ya, it's FAMILY, you stop what you're doing and help." So, we ask, you'd get in your car and go get them or tow their car? "I'd leave right NOW!" How far, we ask, 200 miles, 300, how far? "However far it takes, he booms, it don't matter how far, you just do it. There's nothin' you don't do for your family!"

We giggle like shavuradds and he says, "Sure, laugh, it's funny, huh? I gotta do somethin' … you guys never wanna come around." Oh, that's bullcrap, my brother blurts "Oh yeah, smart guy, Dad fires back, you had to move to Kansas," waving vaguely to the suburbs. "When was the last time you visited your aunts, or even called them. Do you know they ask me about you guys all the time. They want to see you. Ah, you don't understand," he grimaces.

The family can get... suffocating, I say. You don't want them around all the time. And then I realize I've made a mistake, that his appetite and devotion for his family can't be measured. You don't want us living here, do you? I ask, and he almost loses it, because the answer is yes, yes, "I want all of you here, with your kids, in this house, he booms, and I want my sisters next door and ALL my relatives across the street and down the block. What's wrong with that?!"

It's a strong statement, even if it's physically impossible. I realize that he only seems right when someone, many ones are there with him, he is only himself, enjoying life, when there is family.

And I want to hug him because when he's gone I'll be lonely in a funny forever way, but I've never hugged him, not since I was a kid and got too big for that. He's never been sentimental, not even at death, he's seen his share, it's part of life, it happens, though I'll cry a river.

What we have is real, set in flesh and blood commitment, not just a few words in a birthday card. And I know he remembers what we were like as children, that unexplainable innocence and joy you cannot hold enough, fill your soul with, trying to share that energy sent straight from God.

....

But that was then, years ago...and this is now. His bones stick out through that once strong body, tall for a dago, and I remember how his head and shoulders bent and bobbed talking with a cluster of pals, trying to get down to their level. We all must wither before we die.

I give him a little squeeze and it's all bone. Skin and bone... and heart. A heart that keeps beating, pulling love in, still sending love out. I don't know how many times I drove away from that place with tears in my eyes, knowing it's not the fancy things that matter but the people in your life.

"Ay, he sighs, you're gonna have to cook the eggs today. I can't get up."
Any day, Pa, any day.

Dream of Dad

You will love me so much
When I get very old
That it will hurt.

The effort it takes me
To push my bent and wasted
Body and remain alert
Will make you weep.

You know I will go on
Like a stubborn mule
Until I can go no more.

The sweet nut of life
I chew
Will finally crumble
And let go

And combust
Into a shadow
Of dazzling white

Full of mercy
Full of grace
Full of light.

Ci Vediamo Presto
(We will see each other soon)

I will see you tonight
Oh mother   oh father
Ci vediamo presto,

Your knowing smile
Your trusting heart
Your crooked movement
Through difficulty

Arriving sideways
But at your destination
Your proud, resigned face
To sadness

I will talk to you soon
Hold your warm hands
Know the depth of your eyes

Smell the life that keeps
Creating, that fights to
Accept death's verdict.

I will sit with you
On the grandest porch
And watch the world go by

And offer our opinion
On everything
Under the sun and moon.

I will see you tonight,
Oh mother   oh father
In my dreams,
ci vediamo presto.

Ti Benedic'

Somebody's drinking wine,
Somebody's playing moda,
And they're happy.

And somebody's layin' in bed
Dying of cancer asking,
why God, why?

We know there is no answer
Only the straight face in the mirror
A sudden tickle of fear

And we say, make it quick
Make it clean, a
Blade between the ribs

Let me leave this old body
worn-out flesh and bone machine

But until then….. I'll sing… and I'll dance
Throw my fingers, on the wicked chance
That you will hear my laughter

And bless me
With one more
Sweet and terrible day.

Clyde's 75th

Okay, listen carefully, I don't wanna have to repeat this. Clyde is my Dad's cousin. They used to call him Pee-wee because he was so small when he was born that they put him in a shoebox tucked in the dresser drawer.

It's his 75th birthday. There's a celebration at his boutique winery where he busts ass after a life of farming and landscaping. We're drinking wine and eating hot pepper sandwiches expertly prepared by his wife, June. His cousins, Ralph and Bobby are there. That makes them our cousins, in a way.

"How's farming", Dad asks them, an innocent icebreaker? Ralph drops his head and shakes it slowly, back and forth, no no no, with that blend of ancient fury and despair all peasants possess. "You can't make a living farming," he utters painfully, as if he's been shot.

Bobby's big blue eyes bug out as he screams, "Madone' a mi, dage, you can't hire a Mexican for ten, twelve dollars an hour. They won't do it! They got too many other jobs, Ming! Then Ralph and Bobby look at each other and explode, laughing like mad men, long deep and hard. "Come out on President's Day. We're auctioning off all the equipment."

"Settazang'", Dad says, as Clyde plops into a chair next to him, exhausted, and they begin to catch up. "The hell with these people, you better start relaxing." As he's gotten old, Dad is always remonstrating anyone younger to relax, as if that is the golden road. "I can't," Peewee says, "my wife won't let me." "Oh, bullshit", yells Ralph, "you do just what the hell you please." Clyde knows it's true. "Yeah, Uncle Mike, we used to get a dollar a bushel for peppers. Now, it's a dollar apiece. My dad would load up the old truck and we'd go down to the market. He never did learn to read or write. He had a cigar box. He said, Pee-Wee, how much we got in there? Twenty-eight dollars, I says. I thought we were rich. No, my dad says, we don't have twenty-eight dollars. I had to pay the help, I had to buy gas. We got eleven dollars. But we done good, we got eleven dollars. Last year we made three thousand. We done good. "

Immediately, one smartass after another approaches, makes eye contact, and starts throwing fingers, yelling numbers, challenging Clyde into action. Hey, it's fun to screw with Clyde, especially after a long day. "Cin-que! Seiiii! Looking up from his seat, Clyde waves another one off with a dismissive look.
"They can't beat me, I learned from the best, right, Uncle Mike, we learned from the best." That would be the legendary Zi Kite, Clyde's father, Dad's uncle, wine-maker, partier, Morra guru, healthy until his last, sudden breath. When the boys came home from World War Two, he ran out of the field, cleared the front room and rolled in a big barrel of vino. Cousin Roxie, a Marine, shot the pig between the eyes but it took off running. "How the hell did you boys win the war", Kite had to ask? They butchered that pig and the fun started.

Outside in the cold, cousin Rocco asks Ralphie if he can drive. Ralph peers over his glasses and gray goatee, lights a smoke and gives Rock the eye. "Ro-cco...", he exhales, "I'm the only man alive who ever outdrank your uncle." Rocco is stunned. "Uncle Clydie! Nooo!"

"Ming!" snaps Ralph, "I sure as hell did." And he takes a deep drag. "It was about midnight. I was walkin' out of Gaetano's, no action. And in comes PeeWee. "Peewee", I say, "I gotta go, I'm passin' out." But meh... your uncle gives me that dead Indian stare, you know what I mean, and he says....No..... no.... You're not goin' anywhere. We're gonna sit right here and drink some whiskey."

I could just see Peewee's killer shark smile, black pupils gleaming from the bloodshot whites of his eyes, like Sitting Bull on acid. "Madone' a mi, dage," Ralph hisses, "so we sit, me with a bottle of Johnny and him a bottle of Crown, drink for drink, back and forth, until they was gone. I start to get up but he barks, "A spet!", and orders a bottle of B&B, the son of a bitch.

Half way through that bottle, in the middle of a sentence, boom! His head hits the table." Ralph pauses for effect, takes a puff. "I got up and stumbled out. How I got home, I don't know, and I was livin' in Fort Lupton back then".

"Next day, the wife shakes me in bed and says, 'It's June', and hands me the phone. "Oh, shit, I'm thinkin', here we go.

"Hey Ralph", she starts, " I found my husband face down in the driveway this morning, car door wide open." Ralph's eyes open wide. "Oh, yeah", I says to her….. "what'd you do with 'im?"

"I left him layin' there" she yells……."whatta you think, you're the only one can play that game!?" And she laughed and laughed"…..

And we laughed …and laughed… so hard it hurt, and Ralph howled, "Madone a mi, dage, ming!!"

Denver 1963

You sit in front of the buzzing TV
Watching the vertical bars, waiting
For the indian chief to appear

Calculating what cartoon might be decent
And which will bore you to death,
Mourning the loss of your toy soldier wars

Oh, those were the good old days, that list
Of secrets you would never forget, the keys
To the universe that you lost one by one

Along with every shred of innocence, those
Rambling bike rides to nowhere, to the edge
Of the city or down to the Platte, that

Jealous ache at the kid who got the first bike
And his mom said no one could ride it, what
A rat, he'd broken the neighborhood code

And finally you guilted your folks into that ultimate
Christmas gift and now it lay shiny and useless,
You were too old to ride, not cool, must WALK from
One end of the Northside to the other, for no reason,

Other than boredom or a mystery girl and
Too shy to enchant the ladies except for one
Talkative lothario, stopping at various aunts' homes for

Water and snacks, cruising the alleys with their overwhelming
Aroma of lilacs, munching sweet, tart rhubarb and
 Fruit from overloaded trees. Every Spring the short bus ride

Downtown to get our new baseball hats, walk down Lar'mer
To Gart's or Dave Cook's, the only two sporting good stores
In town, once the venerable Golden Eagle closed,
 past the Golden Nugget, bar after bar, weaving in

And out of drunk cowboys and hard living men to 16th St.
Where all of society met, high and low, point to some bum

Holding up a spot outside the St. Elmo or Interocean Hotel
And squak at yer buddies, Hey, what's yer dad doin' here?,
the women in skirts, the men in suits, dodging the mean,
legless dwarf on his mechanic's dolly loaded with the
morning paper, inches off the ground, that he pushed

with reckless abandon, smelling Wolfe's tamale cart,
miniatures, three for a dollar and rolled with string, dropping
a penny in the blind man's tin cup, the sound of poverty,

too afraid to take a pencil, crossing 16th street back and forth
to gawk at the movie posters at the Centre, the Paramount,
the Denver, the RKO, the fancy clothes in windows, the display

of trains and moving dolls behind glass at the Denver Dry,
detouring to 17th, the gray tomb of money, dark cemetery
of banks, over to 15th, the wild side, stick your head into a
burlesque joint just to see how far you could get,

"Get the hell outta here!" the bouncer yells, oh the sweet
temptation, and slowly, inexorably your converse pull you
over to Woolworth's, that oasis of sparkling, vinyl counters
and shiny steel and red leather stools, her bright lights

illuminating every conceivable piece of junk, her giant penny
candy display and hot, salted nuts on a revolving tray
served in a paper cone, drooling over the aromatic pizza
you can't afford and imagining a girl on your lap in the
picture booth, curtain pulled.

Trudge back over the 16th St. viaduct as teenagers race
hot rods feet away, watching out for supercop Buster Snyder,
dusky purple mountains jutting through the sunset, rising
behind the jagged brown hills,

stop to look back at the Denver Dry spire, here above the city,
the gentle slopes of North Denver before us, Amato's shining
statues, cross-topped churches, little markets, tilted flagstone

sidewalks, smell of beer and stale cigars seeping out bar doors,
Tireless, hopeless acolytes, when you're 12, you own the city,
Her magic the first narcotic to run through your veins.

Northside Rules

We wait in line
To drive through Scotchman's
See who's there, look cool,
Laugh at the greasers, their
Insane cars and outdated hair.
Times are changing.

A glint of steel out of the corner
Of your eye. In the dark filling
Station down the block
A tire jack rises and falls
On a lump of huddled flesh.
Whump, whump.

"Look... they're gonna kill him,'
Not with babystrokes but driving
The sledge through the rail of bone.
"Should we stop "em?"
The line moves, we enter the drive-in

In a stupor, laughter dead, snake around.
I lean out the window and try to find out
who's beating and who's dying.
"He deserved it, he's a real asshole."
We exit, unconvinced, drive by

Body gone
Jack gone
All gone

As we cruise downtown
Humming Gimme Some Lovin'
Under our breath.

You had to have wingtips, Bostonians, Cuban heel fence climbers were out. A dark, knee-length trench coat and maybe a snap brim, if your old man didn't grab ya by the collar and mutter, "I'm not havin' no gangsters in this house." Some old men didn't care. You had to wear something to hide your 2x4, yer bat or shiny, sawed-off pool cue. It held a lot if you were a thief. You wore tight, white chinos above the ankle. Your big brother gives you the once over and says, "Hey, high water, where's the flood?" He wears alpaca sweaters pulled up to the elbow and shiny continentals with horizontal slit pockets. He makes an appointment for a razor cut at Fiore's and drives a metallic olive Impala. He wants a Capri bad but that crap job at the foundry won't pay for it. He can't go back to washing dishes at the Marigold but he's trying to make connections to get in the plumbers' union.

"Whatta ya gonna do with this," Dad says, after Mom digs up my cue, my smokes and a Cavalier mag from under my mattress. "You have any trouble, you come to me," my brother says, and Dad screams, "Shut up, you!" I never see my beautiful cue again.

That night, as usual, we're cruising 16th, racing a red Camaro full of fine chicks across the viaduct who we'll never catch in this jalopy, up the hill to Tejon, past the Alpine, past Carbone's, turn at Gaetano's, up 38th to Federal and down to Scotchman's where we wait in a line a block long to turn in and see if there's a space. The Brother Fast blow by with a deafening roar, 30, 40 bikes, green and leather jackets. That looks like freedom. We hear about a big rumble at Rocky Mountain Park and hustle over. Somebody says Westy and North are gonna go at it. Shit like this always happens. Bad blood. Six, seven cars pull in and stop and 15, 20 guys get out, nervous, must be Westy on enemy turf, know how it feels, being the little school when the big boys show up. We wait and wait and finally, here comes a car, three, four, more and more, a long line that never ends, winds around the park, 60, 70, 80 cars. They sit there, surrounding Westy, gunning their engines, waiting, waiting. A rain of eggs and tomatoes flies at Westy, followed by howls of laughter.
Westy retreats to their cars and North guns their engines in an ear-splitting explosion and races off. Humiliating.

We cruise back down Federal to 33rd, turn at Tejon, down the hill to

Olinger's, over 15th St. viaduct and past the bars and strip clubs. We pick up some rubes and this one big blonde asshole keeps flippin' us off. We go back and forth and they pull into an alley and we follow. I know we're all thinking, who gets the big guy, we're all shrimps but Gonzo jumps out and goes right for the big guy who opens his nose with one punch. Crazy Ray is right behind him with a hubcap and cracks the bastard across the side of his head. He keeps slammim' 'til I pull him off.

We're all high on victory and rush to the Beer Depot on 38th, laughing like hell, before it closes at midnight. Don't believe you can't get drunk on 3.2. Gonzo's nose won't stop bleeding and we realize it's crooked, probably broke and we do what we always do. Take him home, one arm under each shoulder, where he heaves on the rug and we panic and split.

At 5 am, a car pulls up and my buddies open the door and roll me out on the lawn. They pull out with a screetch, laughing like hyenas. I try to crawl but can't move. I'm passed out when Dad jerks me to my butt, takes off my glasses and slaps me hard. "You woke up your mother," he says. He drops me and I wake up with the sun burning a hole in my head but all warm, rolled up in a blanket, a blanket of snakes, Snakes!

I scream and try to escape, breathlessly fighting the rubbery, green coils, heart pounding, until I realize... it's only the hose. I drop back on the wet grass and sleep.

"What I wanna know, mister, is whatta you gonna do with yourself?" Dad is standing in front of me and I wouldn't dare take him on. Not for a long, long time. Like never. "Whatta you mean, "I ask, confused. "Whatta you gonna... DO," he repeats in frustration, "you either gotta get a job or go to school, join the army. You gotta do something. You can't just loaf around here."

"But... I just graduated." That sounds reasonable. I'm not in jail, I haven't knocked anybody up. I haven't embarrassed the family. I managed to finish school.
My Dad always looks at me like I'm the stupidest person he's ever met. "Okay, smart guy, you wanna dig ditches, go right ahead. You think life's a party? Dummy up. "

I walk to the alley and try to think. The problem is, I've never thought. Not about this. About girls. About the smooth-talking Casanovas who steal them. About fun, and parties, about sports. But not about life, not about the future. What was I gonna do?

I call Bobby Black and ask him if he's thought about the future. No, he says, but my uncle says I can work for him. I'm thinking some of those numbnuts with pregnant girlfriends must be thinking of what they're gonna do. I call, I keep asking. Nobody knows. Madone, I think, how can I be this stupid. I don't wanna end up in the frickin' plumbers' union like half my cousins, slaving in the mud for the rest of my life.

My Dad's out in the yard cursing the soil, threatening tomatoes and basil. He's got his own little world all set up. A wife to fight with, a lousy job he hates, a house and car he's always fixing, a church, a family, kids he expects to take care of him when he gets old.
He's got it all. Did he plan this?

I look in the garage window at my reflection and I'm embarrassed. I realize the world scares me and I don't have a clue. What... am I gonna do?

Lakeside Speedway 1970

Lying in bed
The sound
Of Lakeside Speedway
Growling in my head

I curse the noise,
The job that I'm trying
To sleep for, then remember
How I've spent my whole life

Dreaming to the thrum
Of the engines miles away, the roar
From the buzzing wooden stands,
As souls in search of thrills

Fly around the track,
Or into each other, wrapped
In a few flimsy pounds of metal,
Skilled warriors and engineers

Their only comfort, a pal's slap
on the back, a pretty girl's smile,
their only company a cold beer
and the big, yellow moon.

Mom's Angel

Mom went on a pilgrimage to the Southwest with a church group. Of course, they stopped in Chimayo. There was a line outside the sanctuary but the female guide explained to the crowd that the muddy spring had gone dry and so the miraculous healing water was not available. The pilgrims were disappointed, especially those who had been praying for help with a special problem, theirs or someone else's.

A little Spanish man stood to the side selling holy water from the spring. As some in the group began to disperse, Mom thought she would get a memento. She walked over and began to chat with the man. "It's so nice you're here, I need something to remember this by", she said. "I'm here everyday", he replied. She opened her wallet to pay him but he said, "Your name is Mary, isn't it?" Mom is surprised, to say the least. How would he know her name? "Yes", she said. "There was a young woman here a while ago", he continues. "She asked me to give you this." Mom is totally baffled at the odd occurrence. "Did she tell you her name?" "No, no", he says. Mom looks puzzled. "She was very pretty, with golden hair and laughing eyes and a beautiful smile. " "Was she on the bus? The tour bus," Mom asks? The little man just shrugs and smiles.

Mom turns in a circle, gazing at the crowd, trying to regain her wits. "She said she would be up at the trading post if you wanted to see her," the man says, pointing up the hill. Mom remembers to utter a weak thank you and begins the short hike.

The gift shop is empty but for a woman behind the counter. "Excuse me," Mom inquires, "was there a young lady here asking for Mary?" "Why yes, she had to leave, but she asked me to give this to her Aunt Mary." The woman hands a turquoise beaded rosary to my Mom. Mom stares at it. "It's beautiful," she says, "Did she tell you her name?" "Let's see, it was Mary, like yours, Mary something-or-other."

Mom walks out of the store, head down in thought and makes her way down the hill. She is going through a long list of nieces and young acquaintances, one after another. There are close to a dozen Mary's. Few have light hair. Her nieces, Mary Louise, Mary Beth one and two, Mary Jo and then there is poor Mary Ann, gone at 35, after a lifelong battle with leukemia. Such a sweet girl. Mom takes a deep breath, thinking, oh well, stranger things have happened to me.

She decides to go back to the chapel and pray, for Mary Ann, for all her nieces, for her children, her parents. She needs to pray. Mom looks for the little man but he's not around. "Have you seen the man who sells the holy water," she asks the guide. The lady gives her a vacant look. "Holy water? Nobody sells holy water here." "But he was standing right there." Mom's voice goes up a notch, as she glances around helplessly.

A small group of pilgrims stand around the hole in the ground of the sacristy, some in silent prayer, others talking in low voices. Crutches and canes hang on the walls. Mom goes in and kneels down before the dry opening, and begins to pray the blue rosary she was given. Time stands still. She feels the small bottle in her other hand.

Without a thought but knowing what to do, she opens it and lets a few drops drip into the dry hole. She feels woozy, closes her eyes. She reaches down and her hand touches water, water.

"Look, look", someone yells and the crowd surges forward, "the water, the water! It's a miracle!" People run out the door screaming the news, others drop to their knees and begin to pray, loudly thanking Jesus and Mary, touching the well, touching the sacred water to their fingers, to their foreheads, rubbing their faces, cupping it to their lips.

Mom is stunned, unable to think. She rises unsteadily and stumbles out into the light. She tries to recount the events of the day but it's a blur.

She turns to walk toward the store, but there is nothing there. She can't believe her eyes, as in shock, they fill with tears.

"Mary, Mary, the bus is leaving". Mom turns to see her group boarding the bus. A friend takes her arm. "Are you okay? Did that heat get to you?" Mom lets herself be led. "Did your niece find you? Does she live here?" Mom looks at her friend's face in amazement, speechless. Mom plops down in a window seat and stares blankly out the window, at the church, at the crowd, overcome. She closes her eyes as the bus pulls out.

"Aunt Mary, Aunt Mary…..", sounds the cry inside her head, as the bus picks up speed and she presses her face almost against the glass. Vaguely she glimpses a golden head of hair, a waving hand and then a cloud of dust kicked up by the big wheels obscures her view and the vision, so close, is gone.

And as she looks up at me with a child-like smile, wanting to know if it was real or all a dream, still she questions. She's still afraid to say. And as Dad stands behind her, shaking his head in a vigorous no, I touch her hand and say, it was real, Mom, it was real.

To Touch the Hand of the Dying

It smells so good
This cool spring morning
Last night the full moon glowed

A phone call stops my
Self-absorbed blackness, opening a door
I listen to a message
That tempts me to be quiet

We saw you yesterday
Your hollow eyes and breathless voice
Promising my daughter a date
For tea at the Brown
Just like when she was a girl

Two aunties lost a month apart, almost all gone
Winter and spring, blood of different lines
The two I was maybe closest to, and why?

You the youngest, you were fun once
Just a girl, you laughed and played
And let me get close.

My mother's sister, you died
Of the same bad heart, at the same age,
And now the two of you
Who could never get along

I see embracing as she helps you
Rise through the sun to a place
Where all, or enough, is revealed.

You are stunned by the light
Shining from everything
More beautiful than flowers
Or jewels, more real than
Any reality you've ever known.
....

We all hold grudges
 Against those who die
Who tried to mold us

 Yet I ask you to consider
 How difficult it is
 To be human
 How lost we can feel.

I ask you to reflect
On all of the pain
They've been through

Forget their weakness
And shortsightedness and
Remember that one big smile

That one desperate hug
That one time they did
 Something right.
 ....
 I've let too many holy cards
 Slip through my fingers
 I want something there
 To remind me of you
 My dark haired auntie

Who laughed and played
Who lost her young husband
Who spoke her mind
Whose voice I'll miss

 My own true blood
 I love you.

Allora ...

In the presence of death
the barely felt breath
of life

What is left   when the milk
is separated   from the cream
the glue that   holds us together
that keeps everything   from flying apart,

The eyes of strangers   that do not see
the darkness   in the center.
Here lies fleeting time   like a sleepy dog
calling, chi 'e, who is it?   this look I give you

When the sun and moon   rise at once
and carry my blood away   your dark eyes say
Play your flute, lonely man   the night is deep
and soon   you'll sleep.
....
Like the insects   that sing
in the dry fields   I sing in my unborn sleep
barefoot broken branches   are burning in the dawn
as I pray for unrecognized desires   for what, I don't know.

We drink wine and crack nuts   complain
because there's little else to do
We trust the angels   to guide our passions,
to protect our beds inside   these four bare walls.

voices echo   in the barren square
doors open   just a crack

the songs,   like the horrible howl
of a soul   beaten into dirt.

You have to have energy
to eat, to sleep, to hang
like a gutted goat
waiting to be skinned

great dry canyons   flanked by standing stones
wait in sun and rain   and when I protest
I am not human   they only scream louder

I feel bad for them   I have no life
to give them   only pain.
……………………………………………..
I belong to no party
it is against my vital breath
my heart beats for freedom
only a free man can be just

every farmer knows   it's wrong to take
someone's land   every walk in the snow
begins with a song.
…………………………………….
Lay a card of St Gerard
on my sick bed, as I groan
my way toward eternity

Let the angels sing me home,
one last time let me hear
the womens' cries and my

sweet lover's final scream.

Festa di Madonna del Monte Carmel, 35th & Navaho, Denver

Tickled by the minutiae of truth.
The sad, middle-aged widow, her dark brown hair
Whispering invitations to the bronze color
Of the men that rises up to the tent tops
Where it looks down, worried, to be
Or to be had.

Bambini in massive carriages are forced through
The crowd of happy, perspiring people.
Some day in the future this child will see
a sideshow face behind a pizzafrit' booth
And think, thank God, he's still there,
This world will never change.

A voice croaks out from the PA, hard to hear
Above the crowd, above the music is where
It will stay. The voices shall see the world
In the church parking lot.

How each one strains to pull something
out of the hot asphalt and pledge to renew
their belief in a light that has passed,
absorbed into the bones, locked in the heart.
....
The statues of the saints are all that is left of their
Beauty. The power they possessed lost in the flood,
Motors and money and the dirty work of survival,
One day at a time. Still, I pray, I believe.

Chanting virgins rent their gowns and bleed from
the mouth. The blood pools and evaporates into
a smoky fog of incense where cloven-hoofed
creatures push wooden boats across a river of flame

Creaking under the load of guilt and sadness that
Arrives with the sun, day after day.
At night, the gates are wired shut and no one can
Enter until the bugle call at the still moment of dawn.

Cheese oil bread. Cheese oil bread.
Patiently tickets are assigned. When there are enough
The wheel is spun and a set of glorious Italian bowls made
In China are sent flying through the air by the handsome
Gameskeeper, he who commands the recesses behind
The hanging capacol' and divulges secret knowledge
To the grubby hordes. I need six tickets, he yells
I got six tickets left and then we rolllll!
....
The street, the burning street, we own this street,
We built this street, who I was a hundred years ago.
Her mirror of loving indulgence sweeping me
From life to life.

I know it so well I must have been here in 1900, 1920,
1940, a mustached man puffing a black cigar, laying under
the grass of Mt. Olivet cemetery. When asphalt was first
poured on the dirty, dusty street, filling the muddy holes

Where boys sailed pieces of scrap wood and their mothers
Walked barefoot and crawled on their knees in procession,
Begging for your mercy, Madonna, giving thanks for
Petitions received. The street is speaking. It knows our names.

Those names go down, down through the ground, propelled by a
Vital, leaden gravity, into the crust of the earth, to the burning core
Where our spirits are melted in the fire of renewal so that
Tomorrow when we awake, we remember who we are.

This is how deep we own this street. If you stop everything
You can hear it calling your name. This is the hand that built
The street, this is the voice that echoes in our blood.

Listen, listen.

I Love North Denver

I was feeling kinda mooshahd. For reasons better left unspoken, I hadn't really figured out, at my advanced age, how to be happy.
Maybe I didn't have the 'ol happiness gene. Hadn't all My ancestors worked to make me happy? Maybe, nobody can teach you that? Oh well, time for a little jittyann round the Northside, early Sunday morning, all the boozers tucked in bed, the hipsters and their big dogs, time to ride the boundaries in the peace and quiet and dig up some ghosts. I can take the highway but the arteries will be better. They'll feed blood to the heart in drops. I hit Sheridan and turn at 32nd, down to Tennyson and Lowell.

Here, in the Highlands, tiny homes for Welsh and Cornish miners, stone mansions for the wealthy who fled, now the Northside's first yuppy village, past Irish St. Dominic's, the Scottish park and Woodbury Library, my old hangout and the jigsaw maze to 15th St., where river meets river and the hill rises to Central, the old shops gone, Johnny's Barber, the hippy hill of Muddy Waters coffee and Amato's Statuary, gone to condos, bars and restauraunts.

I zigzag from the highway to 32nd, back and forth, Past St. Pat's, stare out across Coors Field and uncountable river bottom condos. How many homes were torn down for the highway back in '65, was it? And maybe it's good, who knows, I'm finally past hating all the change and I'm not going back. I do miss Mancinelli's deli, Li'l Pepina's a block down, all the people who settled here, were raised here on Pecos, on Osage and Navaho. Now, their descendants live in the suburbs with me. Think of Grampa walking up from the railyard, the other one loading his horse and peddler's wagon at the market, coming over the viaduct, my grandmas' streetcar-ing all over Denver in search of culture or work. Follow the edge of the elevated highway to 34th and Mariposa, where Dad was born, past Baldi's grocery, up to Canino corner on 35th and Navaho, turn on Osage, past Mary Pomarico's and blind Zi Ming and Zi Indoing, smelling her wash, to 36th and all those damn Marranzino's. If Dad were here he'd be naming all the families who lived in the houses that ran from the bottoms to Pecos, east to the railroad, north from 32nd to 38th, then across to Sunnyside, Jason and Lipan out to 44th and the toolies. It took decades for the Dage's to spread up to Tejon, Zuni, Federal and beyond.

Turn on 36th back to Navaho, Caruso corner dwarfed by a narrow four story townhome. They're nice people, Louise said, wanted to drag her frail 93 year old body up to the rooftop deck to watch fireworks. Louise knows more stories than anyone. Beautiful husband Tony gone, his brothers Jes and Jack. Just her and sweet sister-in-law, Gloria, Scaglia's gone, Volpe's gone, half-breed Gerk's, Walrath's but Mt.Carmel church still there, unless the bishop sells it , growth's all in the 'burbs, no Catholics here, this church the heart and soul of thousands of people still living, the place where grand-parents and children were baptized and sent on their way. This holy, humble place, full of the voices of countless souls, no spirit of Christ here, eh?

There's the church hall and lot where the boys played their own Weird game of ball, bouncing hits off the side of the building That started as a store and rooms upstairs. Those old tenements Across 36th replaced by another monstrosity, turn on Navaho, Camacho's still here, Patsy's too, Pirate Gallery now an institution, Was Levine's department store, the Bug theater, turn on 37th and find Angelo's Tico Tico, a monument, out of business after what, a hundred years? Now, my first home, on Mariposa, the Ainsworth's, Piccolo's, Panzini's, and across the alley on Lipan… a shocker, Gramma Palmieri's, 3733, torn down in a blink, replaced with a giant duplex Worth more than Grandpa made in his whole life. How did I miss that? I stop and stare in disbelief. Oh, the good times, the dinners, the love, all gone, Tolve's across the street, Timber and Slugger, and on one side the Capra's, on the other, the Lamirato's, Gramma's porch-sitting cumma's. On the corner of 38th, the Subway Tavern gone, Grampa's hangout, how many hours spent there, now a café,

E.P. still engraved above the door, for builder Eugene Piro, Grampa's old comba. The Carbone's and Bova's owned it, then a lengthy run of Longo's. Across 38th, Felix Andrew's grocery where we ran our tab, where I saw my first dogfight, Carbone's deli gone, all the shops on 38th gone, no Lippy's live bait, no Labriola's greenhouse, over to 40ish & Kalamath where I swore there was a Swedish church, gone, beat-up industrial garages and fenced junkyards where we tried to "park" with our honeys while chained German shepherds howled and there's the 38th overpass where Pat and Ernie crawled in the
Sewer pipe as the train rumbled overhead for a cheap thrill, by Ronnie Sabell's, where I think they raised pigeons, past Risoli then Muniz grocery, gone, Mariano's gone, Vessa's gone, Rough Riders football at Horace Mann Junior gone, my great-aunt Settafratti's grocery, poor woman, cross 40th & Pecos, Pomponio's and Spera's gone, to Quivas and oh my god, Gramma Smaldone's house gone. Gone. Replaced by another mansion. A wake-up call. Wonder if my Dad knows. All my cousins in the terraces and houses on 41st, gone, Buccino's across the lot, including 100 year old Ang, gone, the Marigold, on Tejon, where sausage sans first became a thing, great pizza, gone, Kate Ferretti, hat maker to the stars, gone, back to Uncle Frank's Pine Cone Inn on Pecos, now another coffeehouse, the VFW, where we celebrated Bob and Maria and many other weddings, where Mom and Dad had theirs, past the old homesteads on Navaho and Osage, Zi Pupin's farm on 46th, the best pizza at Jim's on Tejon, gone, baseball at Remington, that great fight in Chaffee Park, Tony D. and Joe P., Cavaleri's restaurant, gone, Pomponio's DX on 48th and Pecos, where was Frank and Elsie's reception, all gone except for Dad's 8mm film where a handsome young Felix Acierno can be seen assgrabbing and just being Felix. How's it hanging up in heaven, Comba Fe?

I cruise up 52nd, the ragged end of reality, where shabby meets country, where yet more youngsters

pay up the wazoo for a little frame house, built for
three grand before the war, past our personal playground, Willis
Case golf course, down Sheridan to crumbling Lakeside Park and
the Cyclone and once hopping dance hall and haunted Speedway
stands and turn, out, out toward the mountains, so far away, to
my suburban home.

Sometimes, I drive slow, up 32nd, 38th, 44th, down 34th, 36th, 41st,
across Navaho, Wyandot or Irving, wandering from Globeville to
Wheat Ridge, remembering shop after grocery, aunts and
Cumma's and characters, gone and gone and gone, and I barely
know the history and the new people know nothing, nothing and
this is supposed to make me happy? I think of all the sidewalks
and alleys I walked, all the people that disappeared, the days
when this was the only world I knew.

I look for old, familiar faces and places, red lions in
the rear window, a red horn dangling from the mirror, Italian
license plates, even a Hispano from the old days, knowing how
my Dad felt fifty years ago. Forget, and never forget.

I am a tiny part in this human, emotional machine, still tasting
Gramma's ravioli and puland', Frangi's ricott', Carbone's hot
bread, and no matter how many little, shacks they scrape for
another big, new place, this will still be home, this will be
where I feel most comfortable, where my small heart lights
up and beats, where I walk like a ghost meeting all his
ancestors and realizing they will always be alive.

Ascending Blindly

Poetry is a buyers' market
Mary Kay Smaldone

America is no place for
A poet to grow old in.
A poet is not a thing I
Would want my child to be.
A.D. Winans

He'll go a long way. He's just stupid enough.

In This Room

Your consciousness is only equal
to what it can perceive
      Ingo Swann

Surrounded by dead friends
Oblivious to the loving photos
Of family, mementos of small victories

That meant nothing, interests, ideas
And people I became, attached
To by what unseen, mercurial hand.

Art postcards, birthday cards
From the children of innocence,
Pictures of sport and media heroes
I suffer not to denigrate,

Religious symbols of every illusion
Known to man, stones and rattles
And rosaries, holy cards, holy water

Bits of residual adventure and maps
Of unexplored dimensions, stacks
Of spiritual sayings and advice,

Leftover books and piles and piles
Of paper, the detritus of one almost
Used up life, rarely the real thing.

What shall this moment mean
As it skids into yet another
Loss, gain, present and accounted for,

When we are ready to let go
Of what we'll never know

And await what lies beyond
The final darkness, beyond
The golden door.

I have so much

brothers, sister, a father
Definitely kicking, children, grandchildren
I don't see, the dead who live beyond the
Curtain, cousins, friends, acquaintances
young and old, all who say
when a' we gonna get together?

I have causes and responsibilities
Of the future and the past
All from the heart now,

I have a woman who squeezes attention
Out of my dirty soul. I have diminished
dreams and still Kramden schemes and
things I can't let alone

I have the forced drill of limping
Out of bed in the dark and falling
Asleep with a book in my hands.

I have the love songs of sparrows
And redwings, the topless depths
Of blue sky and the teasing ruffle
Inside from watching hurtling clouds.

I have all this
And still I am lonely
And still I want to be alone.

Oh star hear me, carry me
To the very tip of the mountain,
Above glacial lakes and walls of perpetual
Snow, where I can reach up

And touch your brilliance as it
throws out rods of meaning that
connect everything in this universe,

everything to me.

At Julie's Birthday, Ziggies

I don't know what I was looking for.
Waiting, just waiting for my nasty,
Little habits to be beaten out of me.

Kicked out of jail after
You refused to pay my bail
Held out my thumb and a long

Grayhair in a canary yellow '54 Chevy
With the backseat removed, full of
Hundreds of empty Coors cans
Stops without a word...

Even youth can't explain that kind
Of stupidity, the fat file the intel
Squad shoved in front of me

Like I was Al Capone or Clyde Smaldone
Not an injured, lost innocent,
Picture after picture of me me me.

And Did I have access to explosives
And would I sell them and would I
Eat cheese on someone who did.

As I sat trying to explain to myself why I was what
I was, running in the jungle for too many years
Abandoned in the dump of a dangerous mind.

Sometimes I'm dancing   on the edge of chaos
Dancing on the edge   of a fiery pit
Flame and smoke billowing up into my lying breath

And waiting, just waiting
For Gollum to jump up and snap!
My finger off ...and take the ring that makes me crazy
and dance, dance like a madman as he slips   into the abyss

And saves the one
Who cannot save himself.

Follow your bliss and enjoy your poverty

The arts are like a World War I attack
Where everybody goes over at dawn and
Almost nobody lives through it.
            Kurt Vonnegut

We are old, we are old poets
We don't care, we just don't give a damn anymore.

We like to think. We end up thinking too much.
We have to look, we end up looking too much.

We lock ourselves in, we can't stand our self.
We can't stand the neglect. We can't stand that

No one gives a shit about our beautiful words.
We can't stand a lot of things in this life, anymore.

We can't stand a lot of the people who chase
the dollar and have no artistic brains, why can't I

be like them? No, seriously, it's us, we're screwed up.
I don't blame parents, spouses, children

too much or not enough, certainly not the world.
God? Please, I think heaven pointed a finger down

and said, You're screwed. You can't sell, devise
equations, defend the rich or poor, heal the sick.

You get a shovel and a pen. You get to make love
to the angel who leaves you wet in a dream of words.
It's called the Immaculate Perception.

It's called the dream of pain. You will write things
you can't understand, not knowing how you did it.

You will see visions of beauty, flights of sadness,
tribal art and mob massacres, millions lost to mad ideas

how simple people have coped with the insurmountable,
disabling abuse of life since the beginning of recorded time.

You will shine from every pore of your body with the light
of God's own mystery. There is nothing like it.

You have eaten the spirit, your soul is brimming with God.
You are flying far above, a mountain eagle, all alone.

Up here, it all makes sense.
You sink your gleaming sword deep into pain.

You will never bow down to sadness again,
to the voice of who you are. You will never let go

of the angel's tail, you have drunk the blood
of countless dreams, stumbled through caverns of death,

there is nothing left, nothing, only love,
only fate, only the way the words feel

rolling through your lips.

As I Climb
(above Moffat Tunnel, outside Denver)

As I climb, I try
To hear my heaving
Breath, chorusing
With the wild rush
Of the river just
Over the ridge

A mile up the trail
Burst into a cut clearing,
Assaulted by the loneliness
Of a broken down cabin,

These homesteads everywhere
In Colorado, on cattle trails
And windblown farms,
In dusty arroyos and wild
Flower mountains 9,000 feet up.

They lived … here, and why?
To make a living two miles high.

I reach down among
The shaved timbers
Lying like broken dreams
And pick up a rusty nail.

I roll it in my hands
Squeeze it
For life, for memory
Pocket it, this once

The sting of settler's luck
Burning against my skin.

"I Don't Wanna Die A Bitter Old Man"
Don Becker

Poetry is a high risk profession

For some reason, you were in awe of me,
The first and last time that ever happened,
Until we exchanged stories, lives, depended
on each other, until I couldn't depend on you.

Then you looked me in the eye as if it was a
revelation you'd just been struck by, and said,
"I'm a better poet than you", something
I thought was perfectly obvious, told me how
Your madness was real, with a hook to prove it,

While mine was induced by that ol' artistic bugaboo,
Family responsibility. You had a cocktail of drugs
To keep you straight, as straight as one could be
On heroin, coke and an ocean of booze. How could
Anyone so profoundly agitated by the difference
Between good and evil, god and devil, and certifiably

Whacked, possess the kindest eyes of childhood,
Not realizing there is no answer to the beginning
And only a mirror at the end. To watch that special
Mind whirr, entertaining scam after scam, leavened
With deadly jokes, so over the head of the plebes,

Landing you one fine babe after another, interrupted
By pathetic pleas for drugs, for an extreme high, the
Only kind you liked. I gave up on our friendship
Because I had….too many small responsibilities,

It had always been that way and now another moody,
Mooching genius to care for. We all grow up, get tired
of being used. There is no saving everyone. We can
only save ourself. Your two small books and what you
meant to many live far beyond your troubled time.

You were that alarmingly, dangerously good. Now you
Stroll in an Acadian park alongside Byron, Marlowe,
Rimbaud, smiling a holy, wicked smile, you who
saw so much and burned the wick all the way down.

Ghosts
For Gregory Greyhawk

Old ghosts haunt me
In the dark, quiet hour
But this time I'm not afraid.
Maybe…maybe they can show me

Take me inside the shadow of the heedless moon,
Whisper words in my ear, words so much
Easier than the images I struggle with,

Live with, family, job, loved ones
Pain and mortality torture my worried sleep,
Leave me exhausted and sick.
Another gone, the crazy Indian who thought

He could teach me to write, who gratefully
Accepted my beat-up Olivetti as he left town,
Who proudly accepted Father Woody's 20
Slept in an abandoned railcar, ssshhhh,

It's a secret, lest some other down-n-outer
Try to invade. Come, he said, let us dance
On a grand Denver viaduct under a fat summer
Moon and howl what our hearts can't speak.

Let us pretend the women love us
And maybe they do, let us sell bullshit
And pray the rubes buy it, let us
stay up late plying our muse with smoke

And twist the sound into shapes the Lady
Will admire and bless us with a gallon
Of booze and a good woman with a steady
Job to keep us safe from the cold, hard night.

Let's talk about missing teeth, the sly side
Of hockey, why Canadian poets are better,
PR jobs where I made and blew a fortune,
The big scores so close I could taste 'em,

That's why I'm living in a boxcar
Next to the river with an alley cat singing
To me as I cross the deserted railroad tracks.
Here, kitty, kitty, you are the best friend I have,

What a team we make, singing to the stars that
should never be named. Greyhawk, remember…
to forget that name, that you ever met me.
If anyone asks, you don't know me,

I'm a shadow who passed through Denver
On the way to another ship, sailing from the coast
On an opium cruise. I'm keeping watch on the stern,
Where the stone is ultimate awareness as black

As home Detroit and the water is as cold and deep
As Lake Superior and keeps her secrets and her bodies
Just as well. Let us never abdicate our total freedom
No matter the circumstance, we've forgotten how

Important it is, let us be rude and obnoxious and
Craft the most precise and human poems.
Let us spread tobacc to the four directions
And drive our hatred into hell, spewing venom

At white men, black men, red brothers who
Robbed this half-breed of all he ever owned,
His own piece of reservation heaven, and a
Blind, drunken curse on God who stole his wife
And children in a fiery crash, I can't, I can't think

Of it, staring up into endless black space.
You won't forget me now, will you, how I loved
Your simple family, how I believed in the kindness
Of hooded sisters, in the mercy of Jesus, in this Catholic
crap, save that sappy dago bullshit for some other sucker,

somebody who hasn't killed total strangers for a cause he
was too young to believe in, someone who hasn't lost it
all, foundering so hopelessly that his psyche was submerged
in the darkest of oceans, down, down beneath the waves.

I am here, let me speak.

Poets

In this society, the poet, which is one of
The supreme functions, is looked on as the
Village idiot...and, you're expected to do
It without any help.
         Ed Dorn

We are the rock stars of the invisible.
The chroniclers of the unacknowledged

Spirit that makes us get up and
Stomp when the singing starts.

We drill small holes in the subtext of
personal suffering and inject a pain
relieving gel of illuminated sound.

We do all this in private,
In ceremony, because real
Humility is hard to find,
Almost as hard as being honest.

We stitch our words onto tattered
hearts, our tremulous voices leak
Onto scrapbooks of unresolved pain.

We are as certain as politicians that we
are making people better human beings,

That if you peak into my soul
You will be given back your own.

What will they pay us for this honor?
Nothing.
Which equals everything.

And even God eyes us coolly
As we pass laughing
Through the pearly gates.

The Backyard

Sometimes, sitting in this backyard
I'm almost happy. All the painful
Unmet desire to move, to see all
The strange sameness of the world

Dissolves for a sweet moment
As the birds cheep and whistle
In the cattails and she surveys
Her garden, wild roses beginning

To fall, flowers purple and yellow and red,
green and blue names I'll never know, tangle
of bush and stone paths trace a maze
through a terrace of sculptured mounds,

Of lavender and violet ground cover, fox
Yawning on the pile of cut grass, raccoon
Caught in the squirrel trap, the jewel box of
Trees that hides our tended flanks.

I think of the last place, the partying
Single guys with the rabid dogs, the steroid
Felon next door, the white trash grifters across
The street, all the craziness and noise.

Here, the branches of the red plum flutter
In the calm. Something is talking,
Something says to listen, where
Is your mind right now?

A speck of white contrail
Against the dusky sky,
The birds in their heaven

And I.

For Steve Wilson, Artist

The presence   within

Pouring poison   on the liar dawn

It bleeds   on the black

Turns it shades of rusty red

Beginning that should be illuminated beauty

You have turned upside down

Like taking a drink
And swallowing a stone
Seeking that one barstool
That feels like home

Anything without a slick veneer
But a reflection of every edge

Of darkness, slippery corners of dreary,
boring moments when the heart

Refuses to see, ill-thought judgments
Like pale dust, blown by forsaken dreams.

You can make the moment
Whatever you want it to be

But you can't run from the
Darkness or hide in the light

Heaven has a timeless way of coaxing
You out, until you grasp the black border

Claim the canvas of night
     answer the shadow
that keeps calling your name.

I'm Gonna Live... Forevaaahh!
For Lenny Chernilla

He was too many things, an old farmer
who has seen it all, dirt still under his nails
As he's laid in the ground, a retired college
Professor folding pizza boxes for a dime
Who moonlights as a hermit poet

Sucking up the smoke burning off
The pain of a people, of a time,
Of the knowledge inside the furthest
Star and the deepest, shattered hopes
And exhaling it back out to the angels
For safe-keeping.

We dwell in such a deep well, unable
To find our self and asking how does
This happen, this falling into things,
How can they be accidents, and if
Not, why? Just the same pain, day after
Day, when we've already learned the lesson.
Are we supposed to kill ourselves now
Or later, filling up on the habit of despair
Slowly losing the bright moments that redeem us.

We must pick our soul up from the dirt,
Dust it off, laugh in the mirror and build
An invisible monument to our eternal
Beautiful, contradictory self.

We are lighting a fire, quietly stacking fuel,
From moss to timber, in the chamber of our heart.
We are lighting a fire in the lonely debris
We've left behind and cannot leave behind.

We're lighting a fire, blowing on the flame,
Staring into the mystery, the true land
That holds the sunrise, the sunset, that
Holds us like a child, now, and forever.

For Mike Adams, Sept. 15, 2013

What need is there for gods, brooding and trifling
Would any of this be more perfect?
        Michael Adams

Never let the pain make you forget the beauty
        Phil Woods

Mike writes, "I'm an optimist.
Things are never so bad that they
can't get worse. So stop complaining
And enjoy the moment."

You laid there, knocked out
mouth open to breathing tube
Your blood and organs fighting failure,
your marrow stripped of every living cell,
friends shedding an occasional tear
reading you back to life with poetry

Phil trading quips and deep belly howls,
citing anything over fifty as bonus time
and I lay here in my bed, lover next to me
and this is the guilt I first feel, shall you
ever hold your wife close in that
sparkling lovely oneness again?

And will you walk a pine-scented trail
up to a rocky view of what passes for heaven,
feel that thin, clear air pushing open your lungs,
prying open your spirit and letting it fly
to optimistic tomorrows of timeless peace,
dog circling your heels, hawk circling the sky

Will you ever write one more god-given stanza,
symbols of sound encompassing and explaining
all you know and all you may never know,
what you understand and what you might
never understand.

Will you inhale the thick incense of wood smoke,
Savor the smell and taste of what you've cooked,

realize again the synchronicity of nature's tricks
until they confound you into silence and you
can only feel your breath, in and out in and out.

I feel guilty   that you may never live life again
and I will.   And somehow it's been figured in
the mystery, a fine calculation we can only ignore.

How do these doctors and nurses go on every day
knowing that when they leave, tears, confused,
clumsy and real overwhelm the play of life and death.

Friends wanted you old and worthless before you died,
Don't we all until it happens, or crying out with shining
eyes that the angels have brought your father and all
those Slovak ancestors you weren't old enough to know,

yes, yes, it's them, do you see, until you slump
back in bed smiling and in one last coherent
moment utter the words, I love you, I love you all.

You breathe one last good breath of Colorado air
before whatever it is you are moves on, leaving
all who knew you with the indelible mark

of your humanity, a mark they will carry forever,
enriching them, comforting them, changing them
into better human beings.

I feel guilty because maybe none of this is true,
cannot be true, yet I felt it, I loved more
because of you, your honesty, humility,

your blind worship of truth, of the bite
of love, the hand of loyalty, that was you.

Your life goes on and on and not my guilt,
not a song, a deep laugh or small jest,
not a life-changing poem can stop it.

Nothing
can stop your life
from moving on.

Mailhandler's Lament

All the knowledge
I have learned
I could put
In a microscopic crystal

Inject it in a monkey's ass
And make him
An angel of night
Or postmaster general.

So it is written
So it shall be
He strikes his breast
And bows to the pharaoh

The path must be followed
Else why be buried in this
Rutted road he burned to escape.

Too long without a future
That can't exist anyway.
Dead hurt and anger
Behind the soft smile.

Let's bring out some details
About the writer slash environment
Slash nature. Okay, I'm sitting
In a chair, staring at the floor,
Is that good enough?

The pit is deep and bitter
When you finally crack it.
No good reason for this slide,
Aware(ness) that suddenly

You are too low
To get up and should
Have recognized the symptoms.

You have what you are
And that is it. No hits, no runs
Many errors and the inescapable
Path that has led you to
This precipice where you could

Nonchalantly blow your brains out.
Only homemade cooking saves you
From the sameness, the higher
Voice that reminds

Life goes on, that some piece
Of you rests above and beyond
Living peacefully, heroically,
Overflowing with love

And other you's that whisper hows
and whys, this gem, this gem
of an ache, that must matter,
must mean something

to God.

Lee the dogcatcher

Lee was supposed to be an Indian
And maybe he was but he was tall
And there weren't any tall Indians
Around that town.

He'd won some medals in Korea and seen
Three wives go to their graves with
Ovarian cancer. He took my baby boy

in the Stockman Bar and tossed him so
high even I got scared, passed him around to
every neighbor and lush in the place. I was
happy he saw how beautiful the kid was.

I was trying to get off the garbage truck and
Couldn't because it was a sideways move.
I wanted to transfer to the parks where you

could get high in nature's beauty, cut the lawn
And dump the trash. But they had me where they
Wanted me, where no one wanted to be.

There was a position open as assistant dogcatcher
And I took it though the packs of mongrels that
Roamed the beat down little town turning over

Garbage cans scared the hell out of me.
The first day there's two big savages and Lee
Hands me a pike with a hook on the other end

And rasps out, Go get 'em. Terrifying, and never did.
They circled like mad boxers, yapping and growling
As Lee corralled them into the back of the truck.

I soon learned that 7 or 8 dogs together are
Not afraid of humans. Worse was the under-sized
Concrete pound where they whined and groveled.

Astonishing that a town that size could have
That many wild dogs. It seemed that they were
Talking to each other, at night, on the street,

And the discussions were never friendly.
Once a week we'd march a dozen out to
The tiny cement bunker, back the truck up

And attach the hose to a pipe. While we smoked,
Lee told me how much he missed his wives,
How afraid he was to have sex anymore, that
his sperm may have killed the women he loved.

We opened the door and dragged the dogs out
One by one, piled them in the truck like lifeless
Soldiers for the trip to the dump.

A dead breeze lifted as if in a salute, good bye.
Cowboy Bobby bulldozed a layer of adobe over
Their once-yapping, running-free flesh.

I hope it don't stink too much, Lee said,
But I'd smelled all the deer guts out here
During hunting season and I knew it

Wouldn't make much difference.
I lasted a few weeks and took a job
On the only construction crew in town.

Illumination minus one

There is something inside us
That keeps the animal down

Something that loves again when
bloom bites and sighs wither,

that crawls out of its hole
and lies quiet in the sunlight

content to just breathe
almost surprised that love

has not killed it, that the folly
of jammed egos and betrayal

of self has not torn soul
from flesh and pinned it

to the shadows where it can
never experience the present again.

And this realization
Is only the beginning

Before instinct and survival
Before the stars' birthing moans

This dream life but a moment
Sustained by a granite will

Greater than our own,
Propelled by what spirit

We do not know, cannot touch
Our real self, origin lost

In the magic that gives life
To all things.
....

I open my eyes
I am the homesick boy

In the settler's wagon
Bumping down Broadway

The peddler belting his accented song
the sad-eyed silk girl, marooned in

grubby men, the starched collar calling
For injun scalps, the wary eyes of red men

Staring from immortal hills
Knowing all is lost.

....

We are the flowing mystery
Driven from invisible source

To hidden harbor of the heart,
Beyond sadness and revenge

We change   move on
We are the river

We live what we do not know
We change and remain the same

We are spirit
That dares to live

We are human

Sacrament of Blood

I load the last of thousands of steel
containers from the empty yard

onto the pigs, gaze out at the cool
clear mountains and blow a smoke

alone, the way it should be, the way
it is, full of fresh air and electricity

the possibility of life I love you more
than you know, give this quaky,

teary heart, overflowing with ruin
offered on the altar of the gods,

and how many times has poetry saved me,
crushed me, carried me to that place
where I can survive another day?

We ask what it's all about, why each
of us acts and reacts the way we do,

swimming in the freezing waters of
aloneness and crushed ambition

why the desire but not the motivation
to make it happen? To loose the self

from chronic observance of useless
minutiae and lift it onto that higher plane

where the soul sits on stone tablets
and receives divine grace, aching stars
holy flood.

Everywhere I go there's always somebody

Who knows more than I know, has read
More than I've read, seen more than I've seen,
Done more than I've done, has more than I have,
All fine but I'm only human and I'm so damn old
I don't know whether to be embarrassed or not
Even care because really it's too late for me now,
All the changes had to happen a long time ago and
For reasons I barely understand they didn't and here
I am barefoot and stupid and it all spun out of control
Twenty years ago at least and now it's just holding on
Hoping death isn't toooo painful like all the cancers and
Liver failures and old-timers who remind you the golden
Years ain't so golden…

Just holdin' on through a little more overtime, through
The human interactions I'm so poor at while the stack of
Spiritual self-help notes that keep the hounds at bay
Pours out of their fat file and crawls into the boxes
Of untyped poems, the last rewrite of a deeply
Human screenplay that nobody wants, up the wall of
Photos of dead buddies and posters of poetry events
Some I was too tired to attend, skip over Cesar Vallejo
With a sigh onto the shelf of holy cards and pictures of
Loved ones I can no longer see, curls up in a ufo expose',
Exhausted at the thought of life.

Hard to explain how hopelessness without desperation
Can exist in the same place at the same time, but there
they are, staring back at the answerless question.

What I know is
You take the next step
Take the next breath
Until your heart
Stops beating.

Every Day Inside

The big house, the big house
Every day inside the big house
Every day, every day

Walk through that high fence
Through locked doors, hit the clock
One second late and you're written up
Dirty gray ear-shattering noise of metal
on metal, filthy johns, overcrowded breakrooms

Petty rubishots giving orders you've
heard a million times to the monkeys turning
the organs too hot too cold facemask dust
Earplugs gloves squeaking garble
On the PA can't take another minute.

On lunch, walk the 8 foot fence
Topped with razor wire
Chat with the birdies and prairie dogs
Cement walls can't stop them

Stare at the divebombing swallows
Herds of sparrows fighting over every crumb,
The ocean of concrete, the gray beyond.

This is the good life   Men would die for
This is the joke   we've built with our own hands.

Don't let it get to ya,   Don't let it get to ya,

This is the mirror   Of the immortal soul
This is paradise   For the working man.

Every day   I walk into that prison
Every day   I look up at the blue sky
Mountains, sunshine, think
This is freedom.

I worked with 'im this morning. He didn't shine.
He was a dim light on an otherwise bright machine.
John Woods, from sunny Ack'

This bone soreness
Has no power over me
Unless I let it.

I want to believe that.
I want to see the positive
Outcomes of this job

How it feeds and clothes
This idiot's job,
this young idiots job.

Pick up a box, a heavy box
Drop it in the metal container.
Do this every 5, 10, 20 seconds

For 8, 10, 12 hours, keeping up
With the belt. Bend over, lift high,
This job that kills miracles, kills
backs, kills faith, pisses on hope.

This job is what you are supposed
To do, this job is part of the plan
Of why do you do it, a paycheck away

from the fear of survival, a footstep
away from walking out the door,
This idiot's job, this young idiot's job.

On The Road

In the upstairs library lobby
Surrounded by photos
Of old Lar'mer street

Laid out before me
Like a messy, stone white corpse
On thirty feet of narrow glass

Is the original teletype tape,
The holy grail, the quintessential
Emission blown from inner space

The typed-over, scratched out,
Hilarious, heartbreaking spit
On the bar floor, nose hack
Glisten on beer-stained street.

He throws back a gallon of red
and howls at the moon, passing
the jug of holy wisdom,
Trying to lighten the load of

centuries of constricted enlightenment
and release all the conflicted images he
holds inside that think they are alive.

Who am I to speak, even smile
Through borrowed tears
Who trample sacred sounds
With an ignorant northside tongue.

Send me back to the tormented
Suburbs where children sing of
Purple mountains' majesty,

This is no divertissement
This is one man's life

on the road.

WHITE BUICK PATROL

Two old, white-haired Germans
In a white Buick with Pioneer plates
Drive to the New Horizon Church
in the near 'burbs.

Used to be the German Congregational Church
For a 100 years, most of that time in Globeville,
In the decrepit inner-city of Denver
Where they were born.

But still they come, dragging children on a holy day,
Grand-children on holidays. The Grays, she calls them,
In their omnipresent white Buicks, quietly cruising
In the reliable, underpriced machines. American, quality.

They're out grocery shopping weekdays at 10 a.m.,
Dad driving Mom to do her errands, a reminder
That it's not speed but a steady hand (and foot)
That gets you to your destination safely.

What's important is a purpose, taking it all in
Before you're gone, the eternal smell of new spring
And decomposition in the fall, the forgiveness of wrongs,
Forgetting the pain, recalling the privilege of being alive,

Alive, right now. On this side of the grass. With those
Oh so sweet moments of remembrance. And coffee,
Can I get a hot cup of coffee and a small bite to eat?

Awkward Gypsies

At times, I'm an awkward guy
Forgetful, blurt things out, quick
To anger, don't like cutting deals
Have a hard time being right here

Right now, prefer my own little world
Where I am always right
And you, a silver bullet
in my heart of hearts,
when I tell you how you broke it

it comes with the realization
I will always love you, that you
Will always be my shining star
The one that opened my eyes
To the night, so bright, that you
mean so much to me that even
when I take you for granted, I don't.

All the things that you are, that are
Closest to my soul, your eyes, your face,
your contradictions, your voice that still
turns the crank when I hear it on the phone,

all this stability unlocked in mercury,
an element that sizzles when touched to air,
something eternal about us, you and me,
only my lack of energy keeps me from telling

you over and over but then, you can read it
in my eyes. It's embarrassing to talk about
love, to speak the word, two abstract shadows
dancing an unintelligible play.

Our love is like two gypsy moths fluttering
Far out in the Milky Way, strange travelers
Who cannot let go, wondering
If they'll ever meet again.

I was ashamed to tell you
I enjoyed sitting outside
The coffeeshop legs crossed
Smoking cigarettes, watching,
watching.

I had left all the fire
Of majestic dreams
Or they had left me.

It was very hard just to hang on.
Those times when you're
An alien even to yourself.

But my love for you was genuine.
My heart leapt out grinning
To greet you.

I played every part
In the circus for you.
Clown, tightrope walker,
Stentorian emcee,
Fired from cannons,

Tamed lions
Rode horses on foot,
Trusted your catch
In my trapeze double roll

But my favorite stunt
Was diving from on high
Astride the pale pony
Into a clear, blue pool.

And when I slowly rose
To the surface
You were always there,
Smiling, holding out

Your hand to me.

Where My Heart Should Be

I am the sound of my own loss
          Ghalib

The place where my heart should be is bleeding.
The past is planted like an old, ugly tree
In my field of emotion and I can't shake it loose.
I'm doing exactly what the gurus say not to do,
Living in my past and the pasts of those I love.

The angels I took for granted are forgotten, all the
holy ones who looked after me, kept me safe in
dangerous places, kept me pure in darkest night.

The ability to give and receive love was a lit fuse
stamped out. Was it fear or the daily beatdown that
made you want to crawl inside and close off all reception.

I can barely feel the Oneness, the same oneness
I felt, kneeling as a boy, deep in prayer, touched
by grace. It is the heart beat of nature, of life,
Of death, of all that is.

I sit in the fast food place and my eyes water
My wife asks what is wrong but I can't speak.
The children with their parents are perfect
buds of innocence, and I dread their loss, like mine,
their parents' loss, my once great and grouchy
father curled up in skin and bones, shuffling
carefully until his soul can fly.

I think of all the anger and resentments
Between those who love each other
But can't speak, my own son in another
World, my grandchildren far away.

I can sit here and stare at the wall and be happy
and sad all at once and no one understands.
I suppose this is as it should be.
The gray master lets it drizzle until we dream
until the blue lady spreads her soft mantle over all.

Thanksgiving

We have tramped alone
Through far places
Too strange to describe

Where will carried us down rapids
Of emotion and hell waited for us to fall

Crossing unaware   turning points
That spin us in a new direction

Where life always seems to be hanging
By a thread, if you can't stand the living
What will you be like dead

Where despair is like change you play with
Enough for a cheap cup of coffee
But never a good meal

And thinking is a chain clanking round
What is at the center of the wheel

Where feelings are leaves blowing
Wildly through your hollow soul

Oblivious to the invisible
Soaking through all things

Ignoring the soft, warm wind wrapped round
Your worry, as if earth knew it was Thanksgiving

And gave us a gift, let me enjoy this breeze
The blue sky, the quiet absence of nerve,

And consciously, carefully create
A vortex of human energy

That will inexplicably lift me
 into a brighter light

 beyond the sadness of beauty
 and the death of life.

Our Place

Sometimes it's a private insanity
Unapproachable noise at work
Metal wheels and brutal machinery
Nonstop traffic, constant TV, a voice
Sharp and rebuking

The quiet speaks clearly
Says open the door, to miraculous garden,
thousands of hours of tinkering on a palette
pleasing to her eye, where the wild flood

of birds rages in the brisk spring air,
celebrating their brief life with intense
Cattail meadow bombast.

Outside, I realize the time has come
To declare myself soul dimension
Protector of this low wetland

Of the fox and sparrow, rustling reeds
And baby elms, redwing diving at gray
hawk, woodpecker in the old willow,

The inseparable pair of doves that will
Always denote marriage, the wandering cats
And gathering squirrels, grackles and robins

And bright breasted finches, the gentle
Slope of runoff, ever downward to feed
The soft, wet heart of earth and the ancient

Lady apple tree, the remains of the tangled bobwire
fence, posts smoothed by age, that divide us from
Field and pond, here in the middle of '60's suburbia.

From the deck, Buffalo Mountain signifies
The wilderness we run from, and beyond,
Pikes Peak, smothered in smog,

is just a dream.

Merry Xmas

You had put away the bombs
long ago and tried to shuffle
sideways through the smelly heap

But shopping on Xmas eve
You hear a song
And think those thoughts

And your eyes fill up
And it is hard to have to draw out
the knife sharpen it to an edge

And carefully, carefully
Cut out the remaining pain
Even though you know

There is no way
To lose who you are
Or where you come from
Or what or how much it all means.

Merry Christmas   sings the brilliant snow
and crystal sky, feel the shiny goodness
The peace we all desire deep within,

Take all your past and present
and ugly future and celebrate

The unique character of your life,
of all you are, of all you have been,

Hold it before your face
And gaze into its illuminated beauty
Hold it to your heart
And squeeze as hard as you can

Then let the tears flow,
Let the tears flow,
Into the river
of your dreams.

Oh This Luck

Oh this luck, this luck, this little bit
of luck, awake at 6 after a big poetry
deal, lie in bed til 8, pondering

My fate, my wealth measured in clichés
and mannered responses to every situation
I have created in this boring, unsatisfied life.

Force the shadow to rise, not really here
and stare at the walls until noon, depressed
for no good reason, unless money

Family work body brain spirit are reasons,
Too old to care, to give a fuck is what I wanted
to say, so crude, so damn crude deep inside

God what is wrong with me
I'm on this side of the grass and not starving
Some envy my fabulous wealth and position,

My cottage estate, I steel myself against
The too obvious guilt and walk out the door
Into the sunlight, clear and blue, windless,

Mellow today, gentile', flowers smile with hope
Purple and yellow groundcovers worked
From weeds two feet tall, trees and bushes

planted in hard clay, a gentle slope to the water
way of cattails and ferns, none of it can help me.
And this is when I realize something is wrong

Awake for six hours, numb and staring off into
the haze that hides Pike's Peak and floats over a
Flood of green, trees and trees and more trees.

We plant and we kill.
....

I figure the wife can't plant tomatoes and peppers
Until the beds are spaded, so I spread compost,
Dry leaves and start digging, birds carefree chirping
My feelings buried in gray cement.

As I lift chunks of dirt, I can sense
The ground being woken from a deep sleep
Woken and jostled to meet the sun.

The hoe comes out, old soldier of forty years,
Rusted and rickety, handle never oiled, still willing
And the clods break until the hoe falls apart

And you bandaid it and grab the rake,
Which falls apart, too, needs a bigger screw,
And with short chops you pan black gold,

Hear it suck the fresh air and long strokes level
The rich soil, exhaling in and out a thank you
Thank you I can breathe again, and the rake

And the ground and you are one piece
Of creation, one little insignificant piece
Of the cycle of life and death, and you stop

And know the good feeling, shadow raised
And you thank the ground, thank the job
Thank the sun and sweat and generations

Of peasants who unconsciously taught
You how to do this.

Highways

The path of wisdom
The path of work
Lies strung like black thread

Through the limp and dying heart
of the city. There is disease here I
remind myself every day, rich and
poor stuck in the same mind control

Never seeing the light
shining from distant mountains
Bursting out of every muddy hut,
Every square of concrete

every speaker subsumed in bass
So overwhelming you can only run,
Stuck in the blistering hive of traffic,
Seminal noun for motor noise,

Too many cars, we float above like
Delinquent eagles, abstaining from
The chaos of what we must feed on,

Food of confusion and emptiness
Toys for robotic free time
One more dollar to be chased.

There is something real here
In the battle for the buck,
Stories full of living
Pitiful souls singing

A daily song of pain, in love
with what they cannot touch.
If only we could see it
If only we could look

With fresh eyes at the beautiful
Ugliness of death's dance,
At the flowering light
Glowing from within.

Sector 7
For Dave Mac

"I'd sell the smile around you, the quotation
Marks and barely breathing mortality"

In the dream, you emit one of your dead on
Epigrams and I write it down, just like in
Real life. Finally, I realize the brilliant poem
Is not being written

And I roll over, try to write, to not lose it
But it's gone.

There's a truth here, the three a.m. exhausted
Picture of you on your bike, in January,
In the snow, pedaling to work, stopping
For a quick pick-me-up

Right at this moment in the deep dark,
Open to God and acting out all His chaotic
spontaneous humor, your hyper, awkward
kindness sprung from far black space

open, open to all the perambulations
of a lonely, desperate creator,
black angel, too high, too good
for this painful place.

"I think nghtmr chd 26 has inhabited my body
Except his head weighs 40 lbs. and he has
Severe arthritis"

For Og, Grog and Micheline

Lofty angels, cocks erect
Spurt golden sounds of poetry,
Butterflies whisper secrets
Into the serpent's trigger ear

The truths we come to slowly
Clean and clear ejaculation
Of all that forms the soul.

Everchanging clouds
Where desire stands still
Fires holding within
Every color of hell,

And a high one gets off his ass
Stands on the mountaintop
And stretches his hands up to heaven

Takes his mind there in an instant
Where the sounds release him
From the bars of meaning and
Decapitate with one rolling stroke

The algorithm of reason, opens
Our eyes to a music of overwhelming
Love, reaching deep within
Without thought of consequence

And wrap our sorrowful arms around
The pain that has sewn our leaky hearts shut,
Exposing a brilliant rose whose petals

Of rarest silk, thick with caring,
Embrace the last drop of blood.
....
If you stop the moment, if you stop
Time, the invisible world appears

Takes shape in the spirit
Every one of us feels inside.

O soothsayers O keepers
Of nature's flame
O those who live inside God
And see her in everything

O prophets who see through
Sacred flesh shredded into useless ideas,
Into the heart of all that is,

Gallant martyrs, timeless soul
That knows only the invisible is real,
Only the something that holds
The form of mountain, mountain

Tortured, shocked, misunderstood
You are one and many, a world
That lifts and anchors every

Needle on your million trees,
Every foot of your journeyed soil,
Great moss-backed boulders, O

Moles of wisdom as sentient as Buddha
and Buddha knows this. Without condition,
almost forever, your love.

Tell us, Sybil, who stands and sees
Through the fog my life a movie in
The wind as this poem watches now

In anticipation, tell us how the arms
Of God are open, open, always open
To whatever fear you bring.

I sink and rise at once
Drowning in the pleasure
Of the hope we breathe

O mother O father O creation.

Survivors at the Edge of Time

The evolution of life requires violence. And we are at the threshold of vast, unknown territory

Harvard Scientist

There is no distinction between past, present and future, however persistent the illusion.

Albert Einstein

Belief

That these connections
    matter

That intelligence flies
on the wings of the hawk

Carrying light beyond
this valley

  Past golden foothills
  violet peaks

  To anywhere
                anywhere

That love is a force of nature
  soaked through each
    infinite particle
    without name

That touch is the vessel
  of unspoken desire

And nothing can hinder
  its movement through time

Into the heart
  of the pregnant moment.

Heart, Breaking

Easier to perform miracles
In the dark dawn
To travel back and forth in time

Dispensing love to sleeping victims
Inserting wisdom in measured amounts

Transforming the innermost threads
Sewn silently into the fiber of belief

Into the feeling brain that gropes
Its way through dim, lifeless corridors

Drowning in the past, myth of a bright
And shining moment gazing longingly

From behind the cold and corroded
Bars of the still heart.

From the mind...a voice whispers...reach out
Be the sensitive fool, open up

To the golden glow above
To the power below

Let love flow
Unimpeded through

Your empty vessel
Of sacred flesh

You bright light
Of unknowable spirit,

You holy crystal
Of sacred blood.

Day after Night

I am the death carrier.
Spirit brings people to me
When they are about to die.

My job is to love
Care for and listen to them
As best I can.

I find this takes
An enormous amount
Of alcohol

And whatever sleep I can get
When I am not obsessing about
Death, in general, mine or yours,

And finally remember
That life goes on
And I may never know the reason

Why physical endings
Are so painful
And empty.

Day after night
I try to weasel out of this
Unforeseen responsibility

But am never successful
Because Saturn, the old time-keeper
And watcher on the walls

Never gives up
Never lets go

Never takes a day off
And never gives one.

I am the death carrier,
Empty sky in my eyes.

A duality, almost

Death is not in our control
Do you understand

Before we can remember
Water rushes over sand

Death is not in our control
Do you understand

In this temporary clarity
Relinquish all demands

An enormous sack
Pulled over the self
A candle burning from within

Each breath a dawn
A squinted sun
A white bird
Free at last from sin

This is just the edge
Of an ocean beyond time
A deep and loving shadow
A oneness undefined

Death is not in our control
Do you understand
Before we can remember
Water rushes through the sand.

We are such common men
Forgotten freight
In the back of the truck,
Hidden beneath old, musty canvas.

Who would notice?
And they don't.
The truth and beauty of the momentary
world are unique to each of us,

Ghosts songs heard in our troubled sleep,
Where hordes of strange travelers
Move with us from room to room
Uncomfortable with their tedium

Searching for a pure light
We can surrender to
If our will is what God wants.

Life and death, a crooked fence
Meadowlark leap from
To catch a bug, and fluttering
Impossibly, uncertainly, return.

The Big Muddy

The mill of human emotion
is like the horn of the morning train
fading on a cool summer breeze

as it slips through the window
in the half awake dawn
asking you again
if there is a right or wrong

to what is done and gone
a truth in seething anger
a justice in silent need

or only the restless nerve
of this shadow called feeling.

The train passes, it is quiet
you remember
     there is no past
to live in

only the river's constant current,
the boat's ever-changing prow.

After the storm

They don't tell you that
Apocalypse is always personal

That the drumbeat of your blood
Feeds at the unseen hand of mercy

That the deafening bells of dream
Turn the mind as clear as crystal

That the sacred fire destroys
That which lives in certainty

Leaving purity
Leaving chance
Leaving quiet
After the storm.
....

Across that far horizon
Lies the irresistible pull of mystery
Just out of reach
Even to those inside

And just as each cell
In our being screams
With a spontaneous, unscripted joy

Darkness descends.
And the thorn that falls
From your heart is
Swallowed by my soul.

The darkest shadow inside the brightest sun

I lay in this dark shadow
Hand clenched on pillow
Fingers wrapped in sheet

Clinging to this further plane
As if I might be thrown out
Into space at any moment

Every recrimination   of father
husband son, every incarnation
of liar whore cheat

every attempt   to understand
and give, to check flakiness at
the gate of responsibility

every toe touched to toe in bed
night after night, a cinematic haunting
ghosts of innumerable realities that I
imagine to matter, at times, pray to

and all the tribes that might as well be
living five thousand years ago, where
genocide is like wiping your nose

where the 20th century means nothing
where the sinner may be the plumed priest
who'd carve a thousand wildly beating hearts

from virgin breasts in a futile stab at stopping
time, not the peasant who stands in awe,
who senses the inexorable rush of the sacred

passing, who talks to angels, angels light the way
for a young son, steep the glow of offspring's blood
in heaven's healing grace

steady the spoon I'll use to feed father,
unable to speak the halting words we have
struggled to connect with in this one last chance

to allow forgiveness, miraculous dawn felt
in the heart of everyone I've cared for
tried to touch   and failed.

This hand   how does it shine,
What secrets held in its voice
What wisdom gained in its possession?

Is it worth a squeeze, a careless thought
A longing glance as we pass, eyes down
Into the last night none of us know.

Oh quiet now, wise men, leave me in peace
This heart must travel far err it break or confess
This soul must breathe before it finally rests.

Having Given Up

In those days, people who loved Dostoevski,
lived Dostoevski.. How'd Peter die, anyway?
        Gerald Locklin , The Conference

Giving up,   the awareness
of yourself   before you always,
This scent of immortality

You balance, posture erect among the clouds,
the form of beauty   in fragile humanity,
The heart of a monster   needing to be loved

Late, late at night
When there is no one to bullshit
When there is no reason to smile
When you wear the darkness like a cloak,

An old garment you cannot part with
Even though you'd like to try, and the ambience
and easy courage are swallowed whole,

In the sad, pitiful night of alone, spinning
ladders the children of your dreams must climb
to seek for answers they will find
for only a moment, a brief moment and spawn anew
a nest of snakes, a tangled web of struggling animals
that is you.

Then, all light was out
Face to face with emptiness,
Then, the roaring serpent spout
Shot its wad and weakened

Searching for sunny acres, a green
Green place to rest its haloed head.
And will it find it? You tell me
I cannot trust myself.

The House of Death

I have gone to the house
Of death and destruction
Laughing a song of love

A chorus of ancestors
Weave behind me
In a pool of shining blood

Eagles hover
Beyond bluebirds
Who paint the sky
With their wings

Drums drift down
From far off space
Lost dreams
Learn how to sing

I have gone to the land
Of death and destruction
With a song of love on my lips

The children's cries
No longer reach me
Torn from their fingertips

The breath of redemption
The softest caress
Steals into my heart

And the ache
Of all the broken ages
Begins

To come apart.

Mythological programming scenario

There is inside us
this vast void
Which we deny.

Its pretenses are everywhere.
And if we claim the space
where we reach and touch...
Nothing.

Then who lights the candle
in the sudden dark,
Who plants the immemorial seed?
Who brings the dead
Back to life?

Passion meets us halfway
to lost infinities... and laughs.
We burn desire like an old bill never fully paid.

Who are we to welcome the dawn
with absolutely no surprise, no ache of wonder.
And yet, what would a god expect

from a people dropped into a desert
always seeking to renew the flood.
Black scars rush out of hiding

To paint the elements with meaning.
See the swarm of stars?
They carry all the memory

we will ever have
From a place
we may as well

have never known.

The Prophet

You see clearly the glory of nothing,
And stand, inexplicably, there.
        Rumi

The prophet dips his
lonely pen in the well
of blood and watches

Helplessly as the sun
burns it to crust before
he can lay it to the page.

The bird has flown to the
outliers of madness and touched
the hem of she who betrays

An empty sphere of holidays hides
behind a mirage of children's voices
and insults the heart with reason.

Oh where have our lost dreams
taken us?

We have scratched for feed
and pecked for a living

We are warriors laid
low by small battles

While the great war
 rages within.

He awoke from a dream

Of great meaning whose origin
Or end he could not recall

And lay in the clear light of dawn
as one who rarely sees it, usually up
and gone, locked in a gloomy, dusty

warehouse, sheets and blankets
tucked up around him like a newborn
as sunrise grew and eyes opened.

He sipped the morning quiet recalling
the argument with the boss about working
another Sunday, about hitting a clock

At 2 a.m., though millions do it, though it
was a good-paying job some poor schmuck
in Bangladesh or a 7-11 would kill for and

the dream drifted over him a ship of
black sails carrying the dead as they
sleepwalk spinning in and out of lost

worlds, lost hopes, trying to return to
that deep nest of sleep, of contentment
and security, afraid not of death but

of a lack of life, blind tears sprout and
hold and run, a painful flash of how
he missed his grandkids, his son,

a sudden wisp of newsprint blinking
on and off in some dim closet, more
children blown up, little arms and

tender flesh spattered on mud walls,
fresh blood pooled on asphalt,
bright eyes that transmit God's soul,

eyes no longer sharing innocence with
the ones who love them and whether by
bomb dropped from ten thousand feet or
laid carefully by hand, the result was the same.

I lay unawake, crying in the clear, new day
As something inside desperately calls for
The hands of a healer.

Is there not a king who can fix hatred
and revenge and the rational deliberations
that murder not just our body but our soul?

Where is the woman who would touch
Her finger to our heart, illumine and
Cure this endless folly?

And even here, safe in bed,
I doubt the power of forgiveness
And the budding flower of the One.

To Find the Hidden Door Marked Eternity

I make sense of god's nonsense
Put my fist through the imaginary wall
Call down mercy, understanding there is none
I am contented.

I send up a call of gratitude, inborn with a sense of my
humble place beneath god even as I help create him.

God is always a man because on this scale no woman
could be so cruel. See his mother, speaking to the world
Tears running down her face, gutters of human waste
save your Self, recognize the dribble of nobility called soul.

I have no quarrel with modern life, history a disgraceful
Conspiracy fornicating with the one beneath it, tired
Of treason from every authority figure, unable to speak
Without uttering even a small lie.

They say practice makes perfect.
And I have heard enough supercilious advertising,
Dumbed-down propaganda and co-intel to last the rest
Of my incarnations. I've drowned in oceans of blood

These last five thousand years, felt the thunder
of the ages in my ageless bones, the smoking remains
of meaningless battle fought in far dimensions light
years inside the human mind locked in an invisible
ladder of light.

Always we walk the tightrope, questioning whether to
question... Is it our right, our destiny? Were we built to
ask admittance into godhead or are the dangers of
Olympus alien to flesh?

Do we tempt the fire that incinerates, leaves the
soul an empty husk flung back into cosmic drift?

We kneel   and rise

Kneel
                    and rise

Prayer soothes but does it reach back
To the heart of all beginnings
Finger the form of creation, sculptors molding a clay
Whose proportion begins at one horizon
And extends to the other.

To say, I have built the Rockies, I have poured the oceans
That would drown me, kindled the bonfire that would
Burn the whole world down.

I bow
        I kneel
                I rise

Something cries   to touch the face of heaven
Before we lay down in the brown forever
Before we lust one last time.

Stalking the Borderlands

We have tried to repair
The rip in the fabric
Of continuity

It is what we do best
The rest, mimic the landscape
Raped, rearranged, molded
Into a televised illusion

Of what we must want,
what we must need
Crossing the line

Between the obviously false
And the internally sacrilegious.

It's okay   we have dreams to guide us
Locked in gray, gleaming vaults, waiting for
secret commands from that higher intelligence

we acknowledge in stops and starts,
kneeling before black boxes stacked
like giant toys for our pleasure,

entertainment for the emotions and the mind
soon there will be no need to sleep,
the seasons, unreal, the birth of imagination

cannot be felt in any private part
the work of swimming in the mystery
obscured in ambitious trips to Bali Hai,

to the refrigerator, wondering how to feel
something real when there is nothing inside
but loose diamonds floating on an ocean of regret,

baby dolls without eyes
judgment's sharks waiting
for the smell   the taste
of blood.

What is Death

This spiny, smelly thing
This hunk of meat once
Full of wisdom and distress,

Humming in tune with the galaxy's strings
That thing carried by the most pathetic
Clown, cloaked in a mirage

Of argument and hard times,
Deliberate self-deception
And occasional hate.

This river runs in reverse of life,
finally going with the flow
For those who cannot explain
Why they fought it.

Death is life, the life we refuse
To see, the song that sings us
Into matter and then
Into light.

All will be clothed in light
When they enter into the mystery
Of the sacred embrace.

Gospel of Philip

Where the self rubs itself raw
In the haunted smoke sanctuary
Within the cathedral of colored lights

Where we stop ourselves by questioning
Each illusion, inert in our futility
Where the self rubs against itself
Beyond begging for death

Until the relic of bones
Rasps sound into sparks
Symbols into cinder

And meaning flies through the face
Of evil's impossibility and becomes
The bright-eyed child of God

Flesh and spirit resurrected
In the matrix of the One
A single voice like thunder
Peeling from the sun.

you, and god

I am talking to the guy in the movie
I am talking to the guy in the book

I am telling him that all that horrible
Stuff he senses in his soul,

All that crazy pain he feels in his head
All the junk he takes to make it stop

For a moment, can only be healed by him,
Him and God.

He's too smart, too smart to leave, to fail,
too smart to want to stay alive.

I am that guy. I need a redemption
But I can't believe.

Something killed my feelings, aborted
The pain. I can only wait for the sound

Of trumpets and the gentle light of sunset
On the horizon. But all I hear are the stupid

Dogs barking. I am those dogs.
I am broken and can never be fixed

Yet know my seed will never surrender
Even if my lies do. I look in the mirror.

I accept you the way you are.
But not this bullshit.

I accept the you inside your soul
Whether or not you find it,

Whether or not you find yourself
Is up to you. And God. Don't forget God.

Don't ever forget God.

Wound

I have spilled over into you
And now my aching sin
Yields silver to bewitch

And iron to imprison.
There is no running from
The dualities of life.

We seek the deeper meaning,
The reptilian death trance flower
Musky and rude, creeping into
The cracks of our skin,

Into the ephemeral reality
We cannot prove,
Only touch, only feel.

Right now I want to own you
Wrap my legs around your
Muscled mass as we leap

Into a world where spirit
And animal are one, no thought,
No word, not even deed

Just feel, feel
Grapes crushed beneath bare feet,
The smell of baking bread,
The pain you suffer to lose,

The laughter choking in your throat
All your senses suffused in black
Overcome by delirious, dripping gold.

I cut the tender white flesh of heaven
and open a gushing vein
In the Sacred.

Dislocation in the market

This never ending rarely
Casual obsession with the
Machine of chaos and serendipity,
As if by stopping the illusion

Of movement and ever changing
Mask of matter a single truth
Could be found and a correct
Way of existence adhered to.

If one could find it, experience it,
Allow it to come to him, he might
Grasp the origin of meaning,
The purpose. And surely, there was

A meaning, a purpose, yes?

....

The artist in me refuses to suffer
I shall melt into mercy's womb
Obsolete, useless, foolish and poor.

I cannot tell what it is that
Propels me or stabilizes me.
Flowers open to my ever-present

Illness and like anyone made of flesh
And blood I only understand symbols.
There is a guard that stands at the door

To my heart, or to be honest, half sits
Half lies, half asleep, and if I am not
Careful, occasionally, some poor soul

Slips in. With a pretense of excitement
He says, it is the beauty of the artist
To make the invisible visible.

Media based cosmology

This age does not feel like an age.
Maybe none do when you're in them.

It asks for a poetry of computer,
A slick formality, a presumption of knowledge

Without meaning, a deconstruction
That devolves to nothing.

What shall we leave our children,
What shall we tell our fellow consumers

About this time of con men and switched cups.
That we were no longer citizens.

That abuse of money was rampant. We knew
we were basically good, but don't tempt us.

Life was a boring blur. All sorts of experts
Predict some sort of peak or end or climax

Or new beginning when human nature
Points to a slow and feeble decline.

Let's not talk of nature, which we study
Ever more intently, yet know less and less.

Something's missing in the heart. Those who say
they know are fools. No one knows the mystery.

I clamber on the donkey called my self,
Hauling jugs of colorful flowers with me,

And go on my merry way,
Content with the distant horizon.

Pit Bulls at the Yard sale

As if by shrieking
We could love

As if by killing
We could soothe the want

As if by holding on
We would never have to let go

As if through our trials
There were no errors

Not knowing if heaven cares,
Settled in our easy chairs
Screaming at our reflections.

Hosanna, hail to god in the highest!
In the deepest, darkest recesses of the soul,
In the bent psychology of fear,

Fear of death though we do not die,
Fear of everything different,
Though we're all part of the same thing,
Fear of what we do not know
Which is ourselves

Let fear be the ladder
We climb and gaze out from

Onto the endless vistas of adventure
That people our universe.

L'anima

The soul is a gnarled thing
Deep within the cluttered bosom
Can be felt   not touched
Forgotten in pain   or grown large

When the eye lies open
In the dwindling dark
There in the quiet
Rises the silent reflection
of the self.

Oh soul   guardian of the unknown
Keeper of the hypnotic fire
Of truth that burns the space
Between contentment and desire,

Leaving ash for earth, smoke
Wafting through eternal memory,
Leaving light, a gift for heaven.
....
When the priest genuflects
Hands holding the weight
Of Christ's body, the weight

Of all those who kneel and pray
And watch breathlessly, of all
The suffering humanity, of all
Our misdeeds and illusions
Soaked in ego-driven fire…

Press him almost to the ground
Where, head bowed, crushed
He curls, and slowly, impossibly
Rises… lifts the host

Up to God
Lifts our souls
Into eternity.

Inside every atom

The name of god is written
In every molecule
The name of god is sung

When these mountains come crashing down
Like the conflagration in your gut

Skyscrapers topple in a noise that
Blinds the senses you seek to lose

Heaven parts to reveal   heaven   the
wordless, colors without names, emotions
that kill   you can't touch, only survive

what keeps time ticking in the maelstrom
of meaning where meaning is an exploding

cuckoo and words and numbers blow
leaves into bitter air where family
sleeps, waking only to
       ....

there is a golden answer covered in
crystal honey, a bud of distilled essence
living inside each one of us

inside the stillness
    of all things
waiting to be touched
    waiting to be loved.

Creative Destruction

I kick dirt onto my grave
Dream a flower of love

That will carry me to
Heaven when I die.

There are holes dug all over
Erupting with golden light

Wheat heads gone to seed.
I cannot tell if this is the end
Or a beginning.

These are the worlds
I have created out of my desire

These are the children
I have bore through the pain.

I close my eyes and see
The vulture behind the future.

It is time to meet all the people
I have known in countless lives

The voices of the stars
Sing like a children's choir

echoing in my blood, a
Crystal heart unlocked in time

I can see the light must be
Uncovered, layers of earth

Of rock and plant and dirt,
Of lies and ignorance and need.

I see the silver thread I walk
just keeps going, on and on
Into a neverending soul.

Rows of sisters stand above us
Waiting, praying
We'll let things be.

Let the water flow, let
The old and ready die.

There is something inside
That knows, that listens

To the heartbeat pounding
From far out in space.

To suck the nectar
From flowers of heaven

To create new worlds
From a sea of glittering mind

To dance with destiny
Holding wonder to our breast

To be reborn, eternal
alive, all at once.

Ascoltaci

I'm floating on a river
I'm floating in a dream

My mother and father are ahead
Of me, eyes resigned, unafraid

I desperately want to catch them
But they drift further and further away

My grandchildren are behind me
I look at their innocent faces

I must save them, I try to slow down
But can't

My son is running along the far shore
Yelling dad, dad, waving in the twilight.

I feel my manhood flow away
My wife, where is my wife,

I jerk my head around, she should
Be here, next to me

I'm beginning to panic, to flounder
And sink, I breathe deeply, tell myself

Slow down, relax, this won't help
There's a reason, there must be a reason

I remember a medical book, Relax or Die
Dogs are yipping in the distance

A train rolls close by
I try to believe I am sleeping

But there is a hole in my heart
Where the fear pours in

A fear that says when we die
We go to the moon and

Our soul is emptied out, or worse
Filed on some crystal computer,

A technology of pain
Maybe I just don't understand,
Maybe I can't understand, not yet

We all think that when we die then
We'll get it, then we'll know

But what if we don't
No, no, don't feed the fear

There's no point, breathe in the
Endless space, until you awake

Until you become
The undeniable question that

Teases the surrender of love.

The Lady

Languidly, the lady hangs her leg over the edge
of the martini glass. An ocean of intention, of
tentative questions flow from her parted lips.
Is she praying or is she the payer? Do we watch

As she enters the cathedral of superconscious desire
Or is she the altar we offer our spinning energies upon
Where we change bread into golden body, sweet
Wine into sacred blood?

She is painted on cave walls, left a fingerstroke of
Menstrual blood pink sunset on hidden sky, she is
either pouring you a champagne toast or touching
your weeping heart with a fourth dimensional saber.

In deepest black, hooded by light, blood red, blood
red and singing, energy coursing through her body
like light on water, electric flesh chants the journey
into dawn and the beautiful void of limitless possibility.

Yet the longer I look at her the more she disappears.
I wait for the goddess to choose me as her mortal
Mate or did I somehow miss it, for while men make
war I play the waves spinning from her open legs
onto her amber bosom

O lady, lady, I hold a mirror to your lips and seize
the sapphire from your azure sky, a child walking
on the beach, not a care, not keeping score or
squinting at a desolate wall of tortured rock, at
unknown fear that calls in broken laughter.

What I want is soft skin like wheat, wrinkled eyes,
alabaster wings, marble cock caught in vertiginous
growth, shadows of skulls on catacomb walls,
organs lit from within, a hologram of chirping
Bright-winged birds, a highway like a meandering river

An old man who captured the pain and lived it. All I
want is everything, the questions and answers,
is this too much to ask?

And my brain held up by crutches still I seek the roundest ass,
My soul pushed down by the same eternity that raises it I
Masturbate on the decaying colossus of Denver, tied up in knots
Of remorse and disappointment I long to kiss the feet of my stupid

Race, to dip my television in wine and books, until farmers till the
Barren fields to a fire of renewal, until my rod rolls in the tenderest
fruit, my mind in this free blue sky that never ends, just keeps going.

Gently, the lady opens her bosom to the world
Feeds the verdant meadows waving in the breeze
Golden hill bathed in heavenly light, gives her mouth to
breathe the blooms opening to sex, her milk to bathe in

whisper of skin to lie upon, her windswept hills to walk
and from their heights see the soul's departure, she is the music
of nature, where the lonely piano plays, she is the truth
of the blank wall, square one.

We can crawl into her warm embrace and look out through
Merciful eyes at the mystery of our crucified world.
It is here upon her boat where we kneel and pray,
Sucking each miniscule moment, each torment and joy

Into a bottomless void concentrated inside, imploding hot
Silver as we ascend into creation, her compass the source
That sings a heading to navigate the dew fresh day.

On her open water we find her, our lady,
not ahead or behind, but inside
the quiet end of time

The Sun

Started to write a name for itself in
The torrid cielo di domani, tomorrow's
Sky no trickster, full of the native charm
The marks loved, full of herself, but they
Say once burned by the sun, you're blind

So I went my merry way, entertained by
thoughts nobody told me I couldn't think,
which was nice for a change…..a vortex
spiraling from our heads into the mystery
of God tasting of the mental fragrance of burnt

ambition and exhilarated, leaps from the cliffs
of fear, blown by the humblest of humanity,
by the destinies we refuse to understand,

the wound in the side of the wheelbarrow
the way he holds his hat and looks down
the crown of thorns on each head
the thumping drum of fornicating shadows

the handle of the shovel smoothed down to a
shine, the light of oil dripping from the canvas
nailed to this star of night, caught in the
continuum, in the crosshairs of experience
we can pray   we can leap.

We are old before our time, invisible space
Shrinking us down until we must decide
Whether to treat life like a used-up whore
Or paint its magic on our sacred, scarred faces.

The invisible hand that touches the brain
The sharp needles that jut from the ground
We walk, the charge of 60 million buffalo cars

We literally make ourselves into a job, a drab
bedroom, a keyhole, a bored insect, into a
description, an occupation, a pigeonhole, a child,
a parent, a marriage, a disaster we learn to hate.

We make ourselves into a momentary illusion
Of perfection we must constantly fulfill.....
But who are we, really?

When will we get tired of making excuses
For not seeing the soul in the mirror,
The presence that teases in vulnerable moments,
This fading bloom alone in a desert of unexpected
Love, this spent seed sparrows pick at,
This honest rebuke to evil's ugly grin,

We return to the original
Because we can taste the real
Feel the source in our gut.

We are so afraid of being seen
As derivative, yet we worship only parts,
Never the whole.

Infinite variety loves god, yet why do we
Forget where we come from, when will
we tire of breaking things and leaving
them just to prove we're smart?

Knowledge can help you see the future
Only wisdom can help you accept it, sings
The fat lady...and the Source plays a lonely
fiddle as clouds dance a minuet.

Entanglement

Is it so strange
That we are forever connected

That we know that
things
Do not really matter

Let them steal
Let them sow

Let them steal
As long as they do
not steal your soul.

Stripes mix with squares
Angels with devils
Fish with fowl

Constant prayer
Keeps the world afloat
I don't know how

Seeds rise from the ground
As leaf than flower than fruit,
Rainbows blur the meaning
Of tornadoes howling pitch.

Prepare your soul

This vehicle that will
Drive you through the anger
That tears your heart to pieces,

That will carry you
Through the storms that
Torment your dreams.

.44 with a bullet

I called for the eagle and the woodpecker came
                        Vine DeLoria

If thought could have saved me, it would have done so...
                        Pura Lopez Colomu

memory

Outside it was
Cool wet gray
Too quiet, as if a snake had
crawled across your feet
While you slept and died.

I could hear the sound of your voice
like icicles dripping, then falling,
swallowed by a snowy echo, light
alive, asking for more, what is more?

You said you will be here as long
as you have to be here, as long as it
takes for the boredom and sameness
to make a permanent impression on
your soul, a thumbprint on eternity,

A deep sleep of one long golden dream
Of another life full of color,
Full of hope, smelling of spring
Or the beginning of the death

That is fall, like the best movie
You ever saw but more, the best
Book you ever read.

Our memories fly from us like
dad's stories, the foreign words
full of meaning, winsome shadow

of an ancient land.

Leaving Work Early

This is my cave of the winds, where I repent to nature
And the flagrant taboos of society, here outside the
Freezing interior of suburban coffee shop, car alarm
beeping, rap thumping in traffic symphony, 100
degrees on the concrete, slowly peel off shoes, sox,
unbutton shirt, doff hat until I am Crazy Jerry, my gun

the indelible ink of the soul blowing away my own guilt,
judgments, my spiritual death one million and two, oh
look, a stray deer is eating the flowers we planted.
The honorable thing to do would be to grab the 30-06
And put a bullet between her eyes just to disguise this
Illusion of ordered innocence behind the raw beauty.

But no, I'll call the neighbors and start a petition to
raise electric fences around the parking lot. Hey, I just
saw Charles Mingus in the biggest SUV ever made. He
deserves it, after all. In my bedridden dreams he plays a
soft rain of creation, a coyote flute to draw the animals
From the storm drains before the deluge begins.

Oh the desert in the center of the eye, somnambulant
clouds dare to drench the institutional trees stunted in
asphalt, their forgotten names atop Hackberry Hill
where one lonely hack is left standing amid the dense
infestation of pastel boxes, as you rush by with the mass
migration of cars glimpsing the hogback and Pike's Peak
swaddled in soft, sweet rain.

I love sweating from every pore, my disingenuous,
half-angry smirk, the teenage girls chatter, how far out
of place I feel, my whole damn life, in every single
situation, yet at this moment, I am in love with now,
with all there is, right here, in love with cheap laughter,
with looking for no special reason. I've got a smile inside
where it hurts. I'm waiting for a fat squirrel, a pigeon, a
territorial crow or even my domesticated gut to get up
and face the yawning maw of reality. Give me an omen,
throw me a black spell, let my prayers penetrate the bones
of a dead civilization and resurrect nature's blessed curse.

It's Hard

Because you're kind of a mean son of a bitch,
Have to force those smiles, quietly snicker at parades,
At all the silly uniforms we wear on our brains, on our hearts
to conform to our own little group or society as a whole.

The fat lady eats two giant cinnamon rolls
And you cackle. We fill ourselves up   to forget.

Ah, but the hole cannot be filled. The only sweet
filling enough is a little delicacy called unconditional love.

And denied it when young we may never recover,
only pray to God that we might discover

Ourself.
....
Drink some wine
Make the pain go away
We've all been hurt, this is how we pay

Drink some wine until you forget
That home and job you won on a bet

Drink some wine and find your way home
Fall into bed next to someone
And still be alone

Drink some wine, thirsty in your sleep
Drink 'til the tears
Turn red that you weep

'Til the same old sadness turns into
Something new and the same old hassles
Turn a color other than blue

Ride the wild, raging serpents that interrupt
Your dreams and burn the ghosts of dead friends
Who never are what they seem.

Gleason vs Trujillo

Boy, that Jackie Gleason was something else. Did
You know he could drink fifteen Scotches in an hour?

Hell, I drank 16 beers in a half-hour. Eleven in five minutes.

Yeah... I read he ate five stuffed lobsters for breakfast.

I eat five of Casey's burritos, and you know
How big they are. You shit bricks.

Yeah, Hippy, I heard he could eat two
Roundhouse pizzas as an appetizer....

Hey, did Jackie Gleason ever work at the Post Office?

No.

Then fuck him, he ain't shit.
....
I am king of the suburban castle that few will ever see,
but still am burdened by the weight of lifelong peasantry.
Don't get me wrong. I don't mind being a peasant-drone,

have no desire for fame, though a little money wouldn't hurt,
Don't need to run to the track at lunch and drop off my
numbers, then drown my aches in pails of beer or run up the hill

To tempt dame fortune. ...To do a good job because that's what
our innate humanity prescribes, yes, but have never felt the pride
Of killing myself for someone else's benefit, never lived the illusion

of the romantic prole. You could be pouring concrete and some
idiot will blurt out, "Hell, I make more than a lawyer!"
Uh-huh, and you have the silk suits to prove it.

Too old for this routine, where I mutter
"whatever you say", but in the back of my
Mind hides the ever present expletive,
Kiss my f_____ing ass.

No matter how much a woman loves a man,
It would still give her a glow to see him commit
Suicide for her.
                H.L. Mencken

Life is a series of rude reminders
That you could have done so much better.

The road less traveled is often a quagmire
Of deep potholes full of unappreciated advice.

The world that wanted to stomp your manhood
Into dust now eyed you with an ironic, twisted

Smirk, as if it couldn't quite believe what a loser
You'd become. Only dark gods loved you now.

Only the simmering exhale of hell's accumulated
Gases could burn away the web of magnetic guilt

That attracted flies like angry women and the runaway
Mack trucks they drive over your feelings whenever

You're not looking. You used to think you fell in love
too easily but not anymore, not anymore, now

the inviting pink dawn was an unpleasant memory
and only the ever present mystery kept you straight.

Love has Sunk her Claws

And the deep wounds covered
With superficial grace
Are ripped open to reveal

Two bright and frightened eyes
Coals in the dark entrance
To the heart

The surgically sewn mouth
Stays shut just long enough
To remember that to openly

Declare the soul's wish is to free
The harpies from their chains,
Shrieking confusion and regret,

Tearing at the stitches until
The lips grinning in disbelief
Sputter their load of blood,

Scarlet butterflies smashing
Headlong into the polished floor
Another strangling of beauty,

Another misunderstood
                song of grace.

One more time

You shake my soul
Like a sack full of flower

One more time you squeeze my heart,
A washrag rich with candy blood.
I can taste the sweetness

Of the lips I never kiss, an envelope
Licked to my memory, sealed with your
saint's conscience, your smoldering eyes.

Impossibility beckons, frustration grabs
My purple stones, and I'm left with your smell
And that alone kills me. One last time.

It's complicated. He's human. She's human,
We are sinners of a different kind, a species
Captive to every glittering sense, elements

Reacting inside the fever skin, bursting in the flame.
Each sy-la-ble we utter, a starter's gun, timing the
breathless heart, leaving a trail of severed dreams.

I curse at the traffic. These endings, almost uniform
Now, give me room to murder affirmation. If only I
Could cram that cell phone down his ear.

I wish when you hated me you didn't love me.
I wish once you could serve up your lips like the
Sweetest dessert. I am starving, and you worry
About eternal damnation.

It's a two way street. There is a reason we are locked
In this machine gun love. There is a reason we go over
The top, shudder as the barb-wire nibbles our skin,
Face the death wish mirror of honesty and shame.
There is a reason.

I had armor on for you. I was a lonely night of hearts
Weeping obsidian tears. I stole the stars and spelled
Your name with them. Everything was you.

I was sad-eyed Arlecchino, dressed in quilted vulnerability,
You were voluptuous Colombina, a virgin of unending
dreams, a dark joy-child offering mercy, a doe pierced by
her buck's horns.

There is something wrong with me. I want a woman to want
Me like Jaws the shark. That kind of passion, instilling that
kind of fear.

All truth lies white and sweet inside the coconut and I don't
Have the right tools to get at the meat, all balance lost in
troubled dream, forget the sleek bikinis, I want Jaws, I want
to be dragged down

To the deep, breathe the breath of a thousand roses,
whatever it is you wear, whatever it is you are, that's
what I want, you in a wedding dress, me, Ben, rejecting
plastic, breathlessly catching the bus

That will take us to……………

Life Sucks and So Do You

1 pm switching back and forth between
Rush and Andy O's insane jazz, halfway
through day six and everything hurts.
For Lent, I gave up complaining... for 24 hours

Why are all the slobs happy?
Tired of seeing the same stupid faces,
The same conveyor noise, the same blasting,
Fuming trucks, the shoulder to shoulder
Breakroom, the same dirty johns,

The same silly arguments, the same
Avoidance of the spiritual, the eternal
Boredom, to dive in and make love
to the same deadening corpse.

Oh, I know life's a grind, and as I'm reminded
Somebody else always has it worse.
My eyes are glassing over. How do these
People in Bangladesh do it, day in, day out,
How does the shantytown not implode
In a mushroom cloud of despair?

I love God. He exists in the only kind,
Sweet, forgiving part of me. He saved me
From the great disasters only to
Endure the small ones.

this is not poetry, this is self-hypnosis.
What do I know, fighting my way through
Milton, Donne, Yeats and Stevens, not
Understanding a word, a phrase, a line

Until Howl, Coney Island of the Mind
And Preface to a 20 Page Suicide Note
Black lightning to a working class kid
Who hated to work, who'd never
Seen a negro.

Italians, Spanish from the Valley, Irish,
Poles, Slovenians, never seen a real cowboy
Even at the cities edge in holy roller town.
Only on TV, detectives, Ernie Kovacs,
Steve Allen, Mad magazine, relatives
Morning noon and night.

Dad finally asked me what I planned on doing
And I nervously mumbled I wanted to be a writer.
He gave me that queer look that says,
don't hold your breath and said,
don't you have to do some living first?

Can you try to be a great poet, experimenting
Finding and losing a voice, Will 30 years
Of reading help, will 30 years of life?
Is the elemental point to kill your dreams
Or to expose them?

Close your eyes and transubstantiate the
Constant noise into the sacrificial Host.

Get up and limp back to what is known
As reality. Remember to breathe,
Let the music carry you…

And intellectuals wonder
Why suckers like me believe
 In gambling and the afterlife.

Ragged after work
On the highway
Through concrete valley

Gentle green slopes
Shrouded in mist
Rise from range to ridge
To peak like majesty.

This picture is my prayer,
Steering the car with one knee

While I write, as far on the edge
as I can go.
....
Via Vecchia
Overwhelmed by noise
As I try to sort the sense out

Flood of old faces fades
Into a torrent of new lives

To jump into the river of flame
And swim madly through creation

To keep what's best
Simplicity, respect

How you live   is who you are
How you approach each task

Violent morning suckles uncertain
afternoon, husk of ending
begs for a beginning
a still stance in the blur

let it pass, let it all pass on
to where a prayer of faith
replies

For Dana

You always told me the best
Thing about my poetry was
That I had perfect emotional pitch
You stupid son of a bitch

Like I had an original thought,
Like my delivery could save some
Body's sorry ass from misery
Like nobody had ever said that

About a writer, like the sound of
Words was a medicine for grief,
A cold cloth to temper the heat
That burns the soul so early

And leaves only ash, not even smoke.
Lay in your goddam bed and try to
Survive when you don't care and
Know you don't care and know

You can't care, except once a year
When words are so magical they redeem
Everything, all the emptiness inside you,
All your inability to communicate,
To shine, even to whine, everything.

  I am covered in dirt,
  Six feet of dirt
  When they discover
  I have perfect
  Emotional
  Pitch.

Each red petal

In the basket
Like a valentine's kiss
Each yellow sun floating
In the vase, the smiles you

Throw away. If only I
Could cure you, you and me
As the truck rumbles down
The mountain where miracles

Never happen into a bottom
Less whirlwind of ashes
Spinning 'til we fall
From fatigue to broken sleep

Pain of failure in our bones,
The demon rustle of our dreams,
Touching and shoving

Two sailors adrift
And starving
On a beautiful sea.

Cold macaroni and wine
Straight from the bottle
Creamy cavatill' soft
and chewy in the mouth

When the over ain't over
When the house that sin built
Slid down that long, long hill
Desire retreated to the hungry mouth

Slept alone under the cactus moon
Red cock bowed in worship as
the smoky fire's moan answers
the wolf's lonely, hungry howl.
....
Crows flap aimlessly
Against the breathless wind,
Blank pages written in
Black memories of sin

There are those who recover
and those who never do, me
I've learned so much
And know so little

Yet a remnant of hope
Blows regret from pure blue sky,
Leaving only forgiveness
Only this moment, alone and alive

And in the spring twilight
The wind jumps to meet me
And the bare branches
Whisper of our despair.

When You Opened

Your heart to the dark river
Of my soul, the night crept
From its shadow and kissed you

The pale bell resounding
In the crevice between your breasts
Tolls for one last shrouded memory

Tries to remember not to blame
The heat that burns, coos for the
Presence it knows only through her absence.

The bone I carried to you, beloved, is
The spirit buried long ago, the food I need
is your being, my hunger, for your soul.

Day drags into heartless dusk, gray and
dripping with grief, sunless sunset wonders
if luna shall part the shades to show the

desperate flight of stars or
leap naked into a chasible of flames.

oh comet of foretelling, your
trail a shower of fiery tears,

oh dark wine swirling in
the throat like smoke

oh, last dawn, hurry home the night
before she finds this broken dream.

Dark Wine

Uncounted desires
Covered with blood
Lie unburied on my grave,

Dried corpse of tongue
Stone pounding in my chest
One drunk until midnight

One promise until dawn
Wriggles its way
Back into the heart.

Death stitched to
The binding of the eye,
Only lightning reveals

The stranger on the road
The desolation of
The unlit lamp.

Rise, rise
Go and meet the one
Who breaks you

Let your ragged lover
Be the mirror
You faintly breathe.

Denver again 1994

Oh humble humble tucked away in dark corner
bar as beer shots and alley tokes kick the buzz up.
"It's the energy, man, the energy, can't you feel it,
this town's about to explode," he says. And rookie

visions of a new Greenwich, north beach,
Venice west, left bank, Cap hill or Pearl St.
1968, anywhere in timeless archetypal
Artistic paradise of fumble jumble rumble
Hard times but good times oh the golden

Glow around their faces, the moonlight
Over the Platte, the unreal tint of the Rockies
Bathed in evanescent purple and pink and
I'm forty-something and drifting out, every
Decade raises a chalice of dreams and schemes

Yeah, it's all about the magic, the magic of
Work, of opening the door and preaching
the word instead of waiting for the anointing,
a thunderclap of universal approval, hasn't
the Atlantic called yet? or rich patrons from

the 15th century, and by the way, lose the
backstabbing in wasted breath that only
reinforces the image our damaged psyches
leave dripping on the page, not remembering
how this dream was lost gold from the mouths
of those who came before and many yet to come.

The lazy Platte laughs at us, at the reason we
Were born, to live art, why we are here, quit
Crying and just do it, it's your job, never doubt,
Never curse those who couldn't care less but
Bless the dizzy luck that granted you a feather

pen, an arrow brush, a bruised bird throat,
A clown's face, a dancing brain, a fearless will
A bottomless soul, and brought you to the heart
Of this beautiful city.   It happens
When you make it happen

.44 with a bullet, 1993

When we were young the most disgusting thing was older people who tried to act young. They talked too young, walked too young, dressed too young, rolls of fat hanging out of tight jeans or white go-go boots, the bald guy trying unsuccessfully to rearrange what's left of his hair. Why couldn't they just go away and retire somewhere out of sight. They were only good for laughs, runaway clowns trying to be hip. Why couldn't they accept the obvious, that they were lame and out of touch and could never have felt what I felt, couldn't possibly understand the fire burning up the planet, could never relate to this mad rush.

Now, I got the double 4's rolling up like a shadow monster, like the under-taker's dues, like a pistol pointing at my suddenly fuzzy brain, my tight black jeans, black boots that pinch my feet, rapidly disappearing hair, and the hammer clicks once, clicks twice...

Yeah, I never thought I would die, never thought about it, always a Fresh day, a new start after failure, or if I did it would be sudden, now because the future was an illusion, right, there is only now, and the Idea is a very boring graveyard where people spend their lives filling up a lunchbox with bologna sandwiches and twinkies to take to the same job day after day until retirement, until boredom killed them, might as well die right now if living was half-asleep and safe...

Gotta .44 staring down at me, a big silver .44 pointed right between
My eyes where desperation meets defeat and all the struggle to see
The light, to swim up through the shit and blindly grab hold of some
Truth, some art that could save you, verify your life, that yes, there is
A meaning, or no, there is none, but to find the real, some solid block
of God, a deep slab of real that you Could sucker punch and it would
resonate back through you real real real,
And you would know, you would be internally validated like the
Granite mountain before the Great Pyramid, before the skyscraper
That will crumble and fall carrying our secrets with it, that before
man, we were matter, we were energy, we were god.

Yeah, the pistons still charge for every old fart, that's what I found out, that you are always young in your mind's mirror, that 44 sees itself as 18, 20 because you fee that way inside, no matter what the mirror says. But, I'm over the hump, over halfway there, on the downside of death and picking up speed with a .44 staring me in the face, and do I blink, can I go back? You can't medicate the pain no matter how you try, what little knowledge you have is like a pebble stuck deep in the craw and hurting from being kicked in the gut for 44 what seems like long, bloody eons of mental madness and hard time, family time, responsibility you can't worm out of time, not if you want to maintain one shred of Real Dignity and that's all you've got in the end. That you can haul your ass out of bed to start the coffee, that you can feed your kids. Because if you don't the years will box you into a corner and smack you til you grovel senseless and unmoving. Success, failure, you can't tell. Love, pain, who cares. Honesty, cruelty, another stab in the heart. Then you crawl in front of your Rumpole and Abfab and laugh, your Mystery and Masterpiece Theater knowing you would be the stableboy not a lost lord and absorb what you scorned twenty years ago. Your little comfort, your little pleasure.

Oh god forgive me my emptiness, at how I survived the pain, forgive me the romantic snobbery and all the battles against incredible odds, most inside myself. Forgive us our old clothes, our limping cars, our crumbling homes, our mindless jobs that somehow help others, the safety we try to provide our children. For we are 44 goddamit, 44 lonely caliber bullets of a billion billion moments of a billion thoughts, a billion regrets and we thought we would be dead!
O we were the geniuses and we were the saviors, our faces shining with light, hair laughing at routines of every kind, at the life we took for granted, we were the first to reach for Godhead, the first to sink our head in dumpsters and life was serious and life was an absurd game and we were so full of it, so full of it and not knowing it... and we were not the first.

44 knows cheap brandy.   44 will drink or smoke anything.
44 is always hungry now, knowing his soul will never be filled.
44 is waiting to die though he never got enough of living.
Whose fault is that?   44 is expiring on Colfax,

crash landing on Broadway
44 samples all the sweet and rotten fruit.
44 sits like Buddha under the broken tree
with no need of stimulation.
44 is full of shit.
44 dances on death's doorway.
44 can only write in circles, in glorious plum aromas, in navel licking ecstasies,
44 has no reality
44 doesn't care.
44 loves you even if you hate him, even if you young bucks
Stone him as he stoned his own father's shadow.
44 will walk away misunderstood, because none of us tries hard enough, even when we should.
44 knows it doesn't matter in the grand scheme of things
But just the same, like any stubborn old man, it matters to him
and that's why he's writing this.

No one knows 44. They might think they do,
But they are mistaken.
44 thinks he knows each of them,
The tall, thin boy in glasses, the red-haired girl,
 The runaways and run from themselves,
But no, he does not know their soul.

To be sad or happy in Aspen or Commerce City,
In the suburbs or on Colfax, in Cherry Creek or Cap Hill,
In total poverty or lucky wealth,
when it becomes the same
You will need no convincing.

When the hour and the hourglass become brothers
When you can burn your pain with raw forgiveness
When your tongue licks up the streetlight
Sadness left by every loser

Then truth will cut
               the vein you offer
And naked knowing will undress
               and bless all things.

The Noble Man

I go through fever with the earth
Death on top of death, inside of death

Dry, brittle leaves cover her bosom
In a shawl of windblown ash

Old bones crack in anticipation of release
Shadows dancing on the grave, squirming
In and out of moon's pale, licentious glow.

All silent as if waiting, all creation holds its breath
Hums lowly, here…it comes….ssshhhh
Stepping shoeless into the unknown,

see how the light fades, how the barber shaves
the corpse, see how the stucco crumbles in the
melting tongue of summer's exhalation.

The plants give up their seed, the fruit its pit,
The cow its calf, the mother her favorite child.

If only we could stop and breathe the ripe taste
of time, dizzying, a gilt canvas ready to implode,
Tired of the impassable heat, the immoveable cold,

The diseased rain in steady trumpet, one long season of
Leaves spinning round in mad ecstasy to greet the end.

And it fades in the eye, on what is left of family, on what
Was once all we had, the last real noble man, every bit
Of peasant blood squeezed from his pores if not by

Suffocating comfort and security than by the deceit
That everyone deserves to be middle class.

And the traditions, the memories that carry its blood
Forward into battle each day, flag unfurled and blowing
Wildly in the stiff breeze, through clouds of doubt

the descent into mass of writhing zombies, unsalvageable,
without redemption, the long darkness

Until lightning strikes and emboldens a primitive
to exhibit a shred of individuality. And a new family
begins. a new tribe, a new era.

This accumulated despair is what eventually kills.
This willingness to lie down with the civilized liar,
This languorous, spent climax to the act we were

Unaware we had begun, too complacent to stop and
Hold the moment, to elevate the age before it falls apart.

Sight, sight! One clear vision is all I ask before the painter's
Smirk falls from her lips and all color evaporates into mist……..

One extended finger, full of beauty, to caress this
futile vanity, grains of gold mixed with earth.

Everything we're in love with is passing, as the rush of
Past bumping into future roars through the tatters
Of the final sunset screaming now, now…..

Uncertain prayer the only salve to seal the pain of
Layered illusion, if not provide eternal truth

And we are left
                        with the nobility of the soul
That slight beauty
                        no man nor force of nature

Can diminish.

We Had It Easy   1994

They are young... and they are screaming their truth in spoken word and slams. We, on the other hand, had it easy, Free Speech Movement every night on the news, goddam kids demanding their rights but who's paying their bill, what the hell is this, Dad screams, who do they think they are? Red-haired Mario Savio eloquently plays the smart-ass as Dad slams his palm down in disgust, "He had to be Italian!"

I only write this because Generation X is so sick of hearing it, how some silly college kids got tired of being treated like pre-schoolers by their conservative teachers. Or were they spoiled upper-middle class brats. Or both.
How the Cuba missile crisis says we're all gonna die, and we believed it, Mr. Roybal, our 6th grade teacher, paces the class, day after day, covering every apocalyptic scenario. A lying, big mouth, psycopath stands 90 miles away, nukes pointed at us while Russia smiles.

November 23, '63, Camelot goes down, every girl cries on the play-ground, too young, too handsome, this isn't possible, this just can't happen in America, the entire nation in a deep, otherworldly shock.
Then a little old black lady won't move to the back of the bus, a hundred years of second class on a hundred years of slavery, Klan bombs a church killing innocent girls, white stomachs turn and blacks say enough. The time has come. The King is everywhere and I don't mean Elvis. The college kids go south to march, agitators they're called, blacks marching on TV every night.

A half million teenagers leave for Vietnam and a new debate of electronic hate begins. Blacks are burning, browns get down, body bags and firefights, 58 thousand dead young men, on TV every night, not for weeks but for years. Your neighbor, your cousin, your heroes they're all going down. Queers are marching, women are marching, we're well on our way to becoming zombies as the world turns upside down, everyone in the world protesting, dying for freedom while communism, democracy and dictators fight it out, while what's left of colonialism and class leave bodies piled in every part of the globe and the same old people get rich on war and death.

The King goes down, the ultimate black, the quintessential American, the transcendent American Ghandi. Then Bobby, appearing newly humbled. He passes through the Auditorium Arena on the way to meet his maker. The streets are lined with crowds and he's on his way to Washington, I can feel it. Every person in that building stood and screamed. Everyone but me. All my buddies did, who didn't know a Democrat from a donkey. I couldn't handle the mass psychology, though I knew how they felt. Reborn, and not knowing why. Malcolm, my favorite, Red, egoless truth-speaker, straight-walker, another ingredient in the dead soup.

No mercy on the living, either. The music gets louder, crazier, electric, starts saying something. Suddenly, dope is everywhere. For the first time, greasers and soshes, Mexicans and Paddy's get high together, see we are all one people inside, don't have to hate each other and fight for their little piece. A guy invents acid, other drugs, some talk to God, for the first time, some talk to themselves...for the first time. We start looking like mangy dogs, living together in dirty crash pads, hey, everything's free if you make it free, we reject the immigrant, Depression, back-breaking work ethic we inherit from our parents, we reject the class system, the race system, the war system, the sex system. We reject the machinery, the technology that changed the face of the world in one lifetime. Some of us wanted to see what it was like to be really poor. Some of us still are. Bras were burning, draft cards burning, ghettos burning, campuses burning, we were burning, the whole country burning, everyone taking sides and ready to fight. The Silent Majority, our parents, can't understand why we want to change the America that saved their ass, that made them Americans.
Con men and co-intel subvert the elitist movement, Madison Avenue co-opts Flower Power which only exists inside your heart anyway, rip off artists and greasy lowlifes take their assigned place selling bad drugs, "liberating" anything not nailed down, spreading mad dog

survivalism and fear, not to mention "bad vibes". We are saved from this tempest by disco, mindless symptom of a country that shook for ten, long, insane years. It was a volcano. It was a tornado, it was death and rebirth, it was as big as it gets on the mortal American plane. Some head to the farm, back to the land wannabes, growing crops, throwing horseshoes, listen to funky, multicolored blues, a respite from the storm, a bit of peace.

Two steps forward, how many back? We seem to be grownups, without a clue. Why didn't I learn anything from my parents, those hard-headed survivors. They've mellowed, too, their earthy, no-nonsense instincts and big hearts so appealing. Hell, they're grandparents now. But, see, we had it easy. The leaning tower of unspoken rules, untested taboos, all we had to do was push...and it came tumbling down. It was ready. What was so old, became new. But our invention warped and rusted, the nature of revolution and evolution, and we came to realize the problems our parents faced never go away.

What does it mean to be American? What does it mean to be young? To insure that we are free, free to speak, free to be who we are, without government or big business running every bit of our lives.

I feel sorry for Generation X. I hope they can save us, save themselves, bring their truth into reality. But this idealist has seen too much, trusts no one even as I understand their sins. The Big world keeps turning, and what can you do. More people, and more and more of everything.

I still long for a song of hope. We all stand on our own, trying to find our lost soul, trying to light a fire in the ashes of yesterday.

Young Horses

Someone has to make sense of him, you see.
It would be intolerable if he were meaningless

Paul West in Amaryllis

The children of truth go naked into the world

Name Names

*Now I'm dead in the grave with my lips moving
And every schoolboy repeating my words by heart*
      Osip Mandelstam

Yeah, right there
Where I stomp and call names
In the dark, on the back of baby's drawings
Uh-huh, right there, raise the eyes red
To heaven, thank you for one more hokey,
Boring day, for the flawed wonders that
Inspired me to write, right here on
destiny's razor, caught up in the Denver
Dustdevil whirling down 15th St. faster than
A giant urban renewal wrecking ball.

S.A. from L.A. wants to see the "real" Denver
But I'm still bitter, too young to forget the loss
Of all those decrepit warehouses and bars,
All that red brick, all those carved stone masterpieces.
They tore it down, Neal Cassady's block, his dad's
Barber shop, the flophouses for asphalt parking lots
And a few skyscrapers, what's left is on South Broadway.
I don't yet realize this happens everywhere.

So, I name names, Jimmy Morris, digging him deeply
From the back of a gallery bookstore, black glasses
The essence of inner life, like death in a hawk's claws,
Jrm flying up above the gutter, Tony Scibella, back
In L.A. after all these years. I didn't know Italians
Could be artists. Was it allowed? Stuart Perkoff's
Fat profundo beard, reality inside reality.
1970 and I'm at the depth of 19 years of ingrown, brooding
Silence, child of an ethnic ghetto, aren't they all,

Petrified at the utter, artful living of it all, confused by
These hip, Colfax funksters, these sad, funny losers and
High-wire intellects, these gangsters of art.

Some are children of the Depression, but it's metaphysical
As much as economic to them. I always leave quickly, never
Ask a question, never say a word. But...they've turned me.

In isolated Western Slope desolation, my tight phrases turn
From obtuse abstraction to bleeding emotion, flood released,
Still imcomprehensible. Back in Denver is crazy Frank Winters
Heart of the child and my hallucinations begin to become
Recognizable. There's Les Reed, voice of modern man, shards
Of word mirror flung into my trajectory, Jess Graf, gravel of
The street, barfly voice of "been there", Carolyn Baird,
Raising her truth and bringing it home, not only wondering
But seeming to understand, picking up pieces of Loquidis
And Lake, shadows now, reading them like walking on broken
Glass, the page so real it's alive.

Ed Ward smirks at this smarmy eulogy, this twister of language,
Connoisseur of living, chronicler of the Whole Trip, at Faces
And Muddy Waters and Café Nepenthes, they were there,
At bookstores and bars and galleries, they and many others,

They were the teachers, they turned the cold,
they fractured the shell and rebirthed the golden
yolk into a pulsing, throbbing menace.

They all disappear. Into cracks, bars, strange cities,
My teachers, not my friends, not the family
I return to each night in suburbia bought with a
Low interest loan, to my dago heaven,

To what I really want, after bedtime stories and
Worn-out spouse, the small, quiet space where
Rumor, legend and possibility roam around
My sadly smiling face.

And I see them, these broken saints
And between sips of wine, I let them in.

The Man in Black
 For James Ryan Morris

A vague shadow
Stood behind you
Casting a pall
Over the small room

expelling the ashes
Of an old friend
A smokescreen
From your gray lips.

Aren't they talkers and performers
Does it take more guts
To write it all down,
Then get up and read

Or to live?

The way you hung your head
Hung it all out, signaling
In Morris code

This is my life
This is my death

That room was empty
Except for me

But you
Were speaking
To the world.

Do you remember

When we decided to see how many
Cuss words Dad used per sentence?
Two.
Horse's ass being his favorite.

One of my half-breed buddies hits me in
The back with a snowball and I spit out
Goddamit! And from the dark recesses of
the garage, He appears, all shocked and
says, Where'd you learn that?
Why, that's what the nuns teach us in school

My buddy's Italian mom swears half-breeds
Are the most beautiful children, as she gloats
Lovingly on him. Irish men love those guinea
Women. Half-breeds are indispensable, upper
North Denver full of them, Mario, trying to
Teach me how to steal, laughs hysterically when

I tell him I'm considering the priesthood,
Rides me unmercifully when I cop my first feel
Off his sister, then runs off to California with
His cousin, on a whim, all of thirteen.
Oh how the girls loved him. I'm guessing he's
A worn cog in the system, like all my old friends.

I see Kevin's mother, Rosie, at the Feast, she tells
Me Kev has big problems, won't leave the basement,
Will I come see him. As a kid, he'd do anything we
Told him, fearless, 18 year old jazz freak .

Terry, I spy at the mall with a kid, he looks pissed
But then he always looked a little pissed, reminding
Me of men everywhere, of me with my son.

So... Dad's dictionary, every other word a put-down
Jerk fool dummy, in Italian, chatrool, rubishot,
Scustamod, shufilahd, capatost, stroonz, strootz

With no creanz over and over because you hate
Your job, hate your life, have worked all night
For us and now, in the morning heat of the yard,
Beer in hand, our friends all scared of you. Or
Sitting around the kitchen table as you growl,
You guys don't know what it means to be hungry…

How old am I that finally I can say I died for
Your love, your unconditional hug, no
Matter what I was, what I did? But you never
shared your problems and I never understood
that you don't burden your kids with that.

Watering the lawn in the dusk, muttering
I never should of got married, I never should
Have had kids, never bothered me, just the
Fighting. Old sensitive me. Once, you wrote a
Letter to us, and as we stood uncomfortably.
Read how much you loved us and we quietly
Cried, embarrassed.

Now, with my own kids I see how hard it is,
How the time slips by, all the excuses one makes
For not being kind, understanding. Still, I
Remember playing catch, combing what was left

Of your hair, pulling off your size 13's, squeezing
You big flexed bicep, punching the gut you couldn't
Believe you had, and every day you'd say,
Tomorrow I start on that diet!

Once, when the baseball coach benched me, you
Stood behind the dugout, all six foot two, and
Mouthed off in front of the whole crowd and
Didn't care. I was embarrassed yet proud. You'd
Never stood up for me before. It was so out of
Character, you only yelled in front of family and

Later I realized you must have been half-loaded.
It was a funny feeling knowing you were on my side.

I grow up, move away and you become a new person
Low key, no more screaming politics where you shout
Everyone down, try to give me long-distance pep talks,
Make up for years of what you called the Smaldone Curse,
Your explanation for all the misery that beset us.

I'm twenty-five, old enough to begin to forgive my parents
For being human, up to each of us to unravel Saturn's
Ladder and twist ourselves free. I drop the heartfelt

Inner scissors, throw salt humbly over my shoulder,
Say the words out loud, forgive and break the barriers
See each moment, each person, all new. Does it work?

I don't know. There is a lifetime of learning here
A belief in magic, a superstition for every sign.
But I did fly past the past, sat with God,

The stars and infinite space, realized how simple
Life was, how connected, how dreams can give
You the wisdom of mystery.

So, Pops, ol' buddy, I'll take that curse and live it,
Look it right in the eye on a good day and say
Bafangool! language you'd flinch to hear me say,

But then, I am a man, a flawed man. I will
Wear my horn, my hand, my miraculous medal
Because I need all the help that I can get

I will fight my inborn weaknesses delivered from
The stars, I will meet and beat and love them,
Kiss their ass and make them mine,
And I will be the better for it.

The road we take our old cart down and
watch the sun set is the gypsy road, Pa
The hard road, to live it all
And survive to tell our story.

Hold that piss
Find a goddam parking place
Do not use the word inexpressible
Cut the verbiage to shreds like
Other poets backed up against the wall.
Verbiage sounds like baggage.

The motor drives me back past my old school,
Standing in front of the class with my tongue
Hanging out or my arms out like Jesus or kneeling
on the hard floor or playing an imaginary violin.

Touching something small and helpless inside you,
Your mystery. You were more than the class whore,
Blowing all the senior jocks, into free sex too soon,
Not knowing nothing's free.

You thought I was a saint, saw something different
Gave me On The Road, might as well have robbed a nun.
I read 25 pages and quit. Still too dumb to get it.
You tried to turn me on to the Idea.

I lied and said I read it. One year I finally did.
I went back to tell her. She lived with her baby not
Fifty feet from the Valley Highway. She thought I
was a grade school virgin. She was right,
Yet we were both too old for saving.

So, blame it on some divine drunk whose time
Came too late, on another virgin Madonna whose
Brain was screwed by men.

Blame it on the Town and the City, the strain of courses
At North Denver U., blame it on the viaducts where we
Watched the sun go down over the purple mountains'
Majesty and the moon shine on Amato's concrete Venuses

That bless the place where river meets hill, where our
Grandpas worked the railroad yards, where our uncles
Hid the bootleg brew, where they grew their first vegetables

On the sandy shores of the Platte.
I stood on that viaduct and I owned the city. This was the
Place I called home. Those moonstruck statues blessed me with
their reminder of ancient, eerie life.

I held it all in for twenty years, a castout in a canyon of screamed
Echoes, unable to articulate my insulated fears.
I gazed out over the green, jeweled hills of North Denver topped
With steeples, Mount Carmel, St. Pat's, Guadalupe, St Dominic's

And all those Protestant ones I've never been inside and I wondered
For the very first time at my attachment to those dirty streets I hated
And ran away from.

I went back on one condition- whether alone in paralyzing apartment
Heat, young, broke, no drugs, no booze, no job, spinning suicides off
deaf walls, alone in the vacant suburban wasteland that has no end as
Zombie hell hugs me and tries to suck my soul, alone with her
problems,
His problems, their problems, the problems of the world that dwarf
my
Silent moaning, in a green pine glade, burnt arroyo or breathless cold
Mountain vista, in a cloud, a crowd, a funeral shroud, in anger banger
Clanger, in the mist, doing the twist, relaxing the baby fist, no matter

Who what when where why, this crummy ten cent pen will speak
And nothing, nothing will stop it…….

For at least we deserve our tornadoes, a pain all unto themselves.
That pain lays over the city in a ring of sad submission, singing
Halleluiah for the quiet, halleluiah for rock, halleluiah for the tender
Turn of words lurching to their mark, anything is fair game,
Anything can go insane, anything can never be the same, oh god,
Halleluiah.

Another Day

To rip it up and write
In a walking manhole rhythm
Down the dirty, cracked pavement of America,
Small town streets of honeysuckle and vine
Shaded by the giant flowers of the sky, huge oaks and

elms and cottonwoods was the same sidewalk heaven
found floating uptown downtown all around town, the
same grease and grime and holy grit of a billion lives all tossed
together and burned in pagan pyres and backalley oildrums.
Those ashes get us free to flow down the gutter
And stick to the elastic tunes we call reality.

And we are all together
In the patchwork tin garages drinking homemade red,
Riding the tractor through the glow of the harvest moon,
Silent rangers of growth, of death and rebirth,

Organically manuscripted this impulse of ours to grow
And grow, plants and buildings and families,
And we take the time to sit and watch life unfold
And ooh and aah until we meet our final harvest
With no words but tired smiles after all that fight

and rest in the earth, or demand to be burned and
buried above the brown, like Zi Gaet, a new pagan to
name his death, after a lifetime of work, of soil, of love
and laughter and song and dance and morra.

And demand. Life demands you live, no matter how we try
To avoid it. O how we hide from the same old s—t, until we
Learn to live in it and fly not without in desperation but within,
Where the loom weaves soft flames flickering to the touch

And carries you away to the heart of the unspeakable moment
Or the shabby remnants of the past, stranded in angry emotion,
Out of control, where you are forced to look and look and look
Through time's mirror, because that is how you learn.

We are the hunters after sunsets and light filtered through cloud.
He needed to blow on awhile about this whole Responsibility thing,
Like an ill-fitting shoe, striving to make it all work, all at once, that's
All he wanted, to calm not only his fears but theirs, too, to somehow
Give them what they needed if he could get what he needed, the
Freedom to work at this task, not caught in some two-bit shit can job
All right for those pre-ordained but not for him, cut loose as a goose

On a rambling but absolutely certain vision and knowledge whether
It was genetic or prophetic it was internal and irreversible and always
Mirrored the mad spasm and spaced-out reaction to the 9 to 5 energy
Sappers. He didn't want pretentious crap, but to read, explore, look,
Pen and paper and time.

There is a point you suffer to attain
When you know know know
Like you have never known
What it is you are supposed to do.

The arguments cease, the questions die a peaceful
death and you are left alone with that substance
And the force behind it. And you can only wiggle
And writhe and try to squirm it in between the dirty diapers,

The worker-drone syndrome, the tears and screams, the if-onlys,
The daydream brainsoothers, the bills bills bills, and the only
measure of sanity you have- That the universe has spoken
and now you know, and that will never change.

So you laugh and smirk and remain as upright as a slovenly, immaterial
Asshole can be, joke with the old-timers and listen to the kids and
Search the eyes of old age and adolescence and infancy and subscribe
To the earthly news with human pain and honest longing

And hold yourself a moment alone In the rush of your angel,
looking at the earth, a jewel in the Queen's vast blue gown,

    Holding that moment   Of peace and prayer
        And letting it go
            To face the face of another day.

Denver Exile, 1975

Who's out there? I only need your mutterings. Who's waiting
for a bus on 16th, mannequin before a window. Who stood on
the rooftop and saw eternity fading off the wall?
Who got spit on by your dying hobos, a Depression become
a suicide, who tore the crimson crosses from head, fish and
body shops in a farewell reverie to Japtown stuck in a tower,
the sellout quick and cold to growth riot uncontrolled,
Reeling under the deadly weight of trendy crap and making
it in the big city ignorance, bridges and viaducts creaking
under poison alchemies?

What we stole and suffered for has become a strange undeniable
Fact of either accepting our imprisonment or getting out. It's
hard to leave an old-timer lying In the warm redstone gutters
that soaked up this painted lady's aspirations, her erratic
moods and murders, now we're like red men nailed to a
chrome mirage, hoping we can be spirited away before this
river rest Is transformed into an even more alien incarnation.

There's an uncertainty about when the real fight ended.
Or how it even began. Scattered pockets of resistance live on
in smoky old bars, in parish clubs, in any heartstrung traveler who
falls into this town's genuine feel, its shaky-handed reminiscence,
slow death reflected off its glass towers and swinging singles
oases, inhabited by endless grains of sand, buried alive.

Some in their small world target enemy operations and perform
Emotional whammies on the forces of Bigness, then wrestle the
Guilt the guilt of negativity unaware we are antennae and that
Progress is measured within. Sooner or later it gets hard to look
At, to listen to. Think of your mother and father dying right
before your eyes in the most callous, undignified fashion.
The cottonwoods cry is drowned in the din of clashing registers.

So, you build on a back alley between a Cherry Creek fire escape
And the smoking railroad bottoms, staring out at the shining
mountains, dropping leaflets of life down to gasping whores
and panhandlers, waiting for the tip of the flame to burn your
ass a little higher.

For my son- 1

The leaders of the world do not know
That there is no greater power than
Holding a baby until it falls asleep

The bankers of the earth do not know
That the stones that shimmer beneath
The water's sheen hold greater wealth
In their decrepit veins than all the bricks
Of unseen gold, horded away.

There is more truth in one old philosopher's
Naked eye than all the latest computers,
More hope in chasing butterflies than in
The fathers who chase their children away.
There is more knowledge in the flesh of a tree,
In a subtle shift of wind, in the fluid flight of birds
than in TV's sudden, boring thrill drills.

Life in large watermelon slices tumbles from
Grouchy beds, catapults peculiar clouds and
Bodies and faces as all the strange juxtapositions

Go unnoticed, the real real, the channel of public
Awareness tuned out, turned off, dead?
And not even reported in Time.

....

The wisps of spring cloud
Dissipate.
Sitting on the porch
Where I held my son
Curled and bleeding,
Glad I hadn't seen him fly
off the machine.

I hear his voice from somewhere.
The empty blue sky turns around his
infinite blue eyes, two inches from my face.
He is alive.   I sit in the sun
And I believe

2

He is asleep upstairs. I am sitting
In the chair where I dreamt up
My grandparents in the dark and
Took their smiles as approval and

Their remembered pain as a simple
Warning: Relax, and let it pass.
Find life- it's waiting in the little things.

The boy I yell at. Because I'm sick of
Arguing about no money.
Because I know he can take it and come
Back ten minutes later and take my hand

And show me his new drawing, his new idea,
His new invention, these little things that
Totally occupy his soul at this moment, thus
Clueing me in to their true importance.

Isn't that a good excuse to abuse his trust?
Children are the most human of us.
Unafraid to be honest, mean, conniving,
Lost in visions of the future, little rabazione's,

Absorbed in the ever present, in the wide, wide
World, where they can see wonder and cruelty
Side by side. I know my parents would give their
lives for me without thinking, so pure the blood flows

And I know how they loved me, like I love my children;
with no calm, no sense, no badly-needed patience or
understanding, their utter innocent beauty
too unbearable to watch,

I love my babies.
And I hate to give them up.
One last kiss tonight, asleep
for the one who cannot bear it
in the day.

3
He goes running out the door, yelling, "bye, bye"
off to spend the night down the block.
The moon is full, Alissa spins around my legs.

"Where's he going, Dad? This is what a bird's
Wings look like." Inside, I hear the TV, another
prime time movie too violent even for adults.

A jet buzzes overhead. Where are all the children?
Why don't they come out to play? Did all those nights
we begged to stay out, playing ball or hide and seek, cops

and robbers or telling scary stories under the same big moon
Make us better, more well-rounded adults? Are these
Kids missing out, with the incredible speed of addictive

Video games and their true life cartoons that must
Always have a moral? We had the humorous, nonsensical
Violence of Bugs, Tom and Jerry, Wily Coyote, the farce of
Mo, Larry and Curly. Okay, they do have All Star wrestling.

He stands under a distant streetlight waving. He always seems
to be leaving. And whenever he does, I can't stand to see him go.
....
I give you the long tormented rides
Around that small town as I babbled

Anger pain frustration at life, at love, at me.
I took the smiles, the running, bouncing
Young tomcat energy, bursting at the seams
Shining out the eyes too much to hold.

You are my baby, Jes, you are my son.
I know I hold your love too tight,

Was is it a mistake to live for you
In the slow fire of minute hell,
Hoping for a miracle, a limbo for our
Lost souls, a miracle for our mad motion.

4- I am Here
For Ed and Marcia

Someday you will laugh at me
At the secret way I've loved you,
You will understand the tether

holding my heart back, know my
harsh words and lame apologies,
my infinite exhaustion, know my lazy

eyes that can't leave the TV or paper,
know that I miss you so bad
after I send you to bed.

Part of me is missing.
It has your indescribable soul on it.
It is the deepest part of what I love,

Of who I am. It is the absolute
Fragility of childhood.
It is exuberantly painful. I try

Not to put that hidden pain on you.
You, I want to be happy, you I can't save
Only pray for. Only hope you survive

To thirty, because then you'll be able
To tell me how much you love me.
You'll know the torment of guidance,

That there is no way to do it.
You tell me now you love me
But I don't listen, I prefer to

Miss you at work, to recall
The round, vibrant tone of your voice,
The way nothing is serious with me, the way
Everything can be serious with your friends.

Someday, you will need a harbor
I will be in dry dock for the duration.
I hope you will stop by for a glass of wine
To watch the stars come out.

For now, my plans and maybe's don't amount
to much. Now, is when you can sit on my lap
And put my arm around you. There is no
Such thing as spending enough time with you.

I am here.

That's what I want you to know.
Before the jobs, the money, the adults,
The problems, the hopes, the aspirations,

Before the end of the world, I'm here,
A tree, a rock to lean on once in a while
And look away at the horizon.

I think of you each day.
The thought drops to my heart
And floods it, drops deeper

To my gut, where fear and strength struggle
Love and death, answers I don't have,
Beginnings and ends

I am here
And the reason is because
You have made my life worth living.

Even at such a young age
You have worked a miracle,
You have given
The greatest gift.

Premature Mid-life Crisis Blues

I'm writing with this body
Though it may not know me anymore,
With every painful moral stance

And each vanishing apparition, with
Every burst of unemployment, every
Stale cracker, every jerk-off foreman

I'm writing with every mortgage payment
Because I love my brood and know
Their needs, too tired to read, too late

To free my body as the spirit carries on
And the mind bullshits with coworkers,
All caught in the charade.

Some take it heavy, the unattached take
It easy, I take it and spit it back,
I gave my guts to writing, gave my

Bloody dreams, my shoulders to insanities,
What will one more hurt. I got back
Half a heart, teeth marks riveted on the edge,

A brain beset with economic tragedy, just a
security-minded worker drone and a family
to settle the panic they helped instigate.

I'm writing with this body, laying it on the line
The chalk line that says I'm plumb and level,
The baseline the children run in tattered

Tennis shoes, the chorus line tripping my every
Move in the spotlight, the thin red line,
The line of tracks chugging me to sleep,

The straight and narrow, fly like and arrow
Do it right and maybe tonight, you'll write.

The Last Jew

Well, there he was, the last jew.
They couldn't decide what to do with him.
Starve him? Beat him as he's led toward a deep pit

full of the blood and excrement and dried bones of
his brothers and sisters? Whip him into shreds of flesh
so carrion birds can pick at his gut strings, oh what music,

will the chosen people still carry the celestial ecstasy in
their genes, will the wanderering tormented finally make
everyone happy by being transported to heavenly blue,
far from this millennial penance of humiliating abuse?

Maybe we shall lie to him, offer an outstretched hand of hope,
fool him right up until the moment the gas is turned on and he
is washed of all humanity, or wait, there must be one last jew to

Torture for eternity, does not our faith demand it, are they not
guilty of any number of silly, unbelievable conspiracies and who
will take the blame for the Blame when the last jew is gone? Hmmm

As the clean blade slices through his neck and we are at last
liberated from jewish lies and persecutions we shall be so happy,
The way made clear for a bloody savior. The jew will push

on the walls of heaven, testing his faith, his simple thirst for truth
and acceptance of mystery, to overcome despair in a vision of God,
to validate life in this imminent death, to be able to say yes,

Life has a purpose, not all men are evil, corrupt and stupid. Shall
he attack, lash out at the end, take a life for his own, for his race.
Over the crowd, you can hear a scream as he relieves thousands
of years of persecution, as he decides to sit quietly with dignity

and dies, like millions of others, of every race and color, thrown
into the fire and let me see if the demons who twist the sacred
with eyes which cannot understand can catch him as he rises.

The Placebo Effect

The shadow of guilty intelligence
Flickers from the biped's stealthy passing

As if they knew   they were special
But could not figure out   how   or why

And so, in the best tradition, destroyed
Even as they created.

The jungle smiles   the tundra sings
The caribou and zebra   share
A silent knowing

Only we   do not understand

Only we   build castles hoping
To find a soul   enslave a world
To pass the time

Oh big, we think big
Abusing every lightbulb squeezed
from a garret geniuses sad, pathetic life
turning sacramental artifacts into
consumer sales...

and   I forgive
forgive it all

we are makers, thinkers, connivers
we can't help it, we were meant to

even the cathedrals of shame filled to their
illumined heights with the bones of ignorance

only a testament to how we craved a respite
from the black night, quivered at the stroke
of the thunderbird's wing

lost in nature's scope and immensity, giving
names to powers we could not possibly understand.

We did all right. We didn't completely
exterminate everyone. The bugs are still here,
the stars spinning closer and from their forges
flinging angry bits of fiery dust still gleam like
our deepest dream, our salvation, our home.

Exhale   and give birth
to this history scientists say doesn't exist
except in parallel realities

You will never be smart enough,
Kind enough, vicious enough, wise enough
To resurrect our forgotten destiny…
Or to obliterate the numbing pain.

Sit back   and enjoy the ride

Up there   around the bend

Is the unexpected

Unfolding in every living thing.

Live   live
          Until you die.

What the Mountain Tells Me

In every bite of chocolate there is love.
It is not just what you feel
It is what the chocolate tells you

Its essence fills rivers with desire
Floods the long dormant plain, its name
Is memory, eons old, its breath is a shallow

Panting, light sweat, rose cheeks, on top of
The chocolate is the scent, vanilla, cinnamon
Honey, berries, leather, mossy wood.

The most exotic blossoms give their glories
To the Sun, the entrance to the beyond
Between two sheets, two blades of grass

Sun melts snow in a low moan
Scent of spring's eternal return
Releases an avalanche of sound

A trickling brook cuts through glacial wild
Flowers, new sprouts, mountain flexes loins
Feels its own power, with a roar looses its

Restrained need onto animal slumber, blushing
Virgin overwhelmed by ice, then heat,
By fresh color, aromas tingling every sense.

From chocolate comes the fruit of paradise
What begins with desire is completed in the seed.

And the cycle sings its song of
Blackest night and brightest dawn
Living light carried on waves of space
And what we eat is the sweetest grace.

The Game

The sky blue breeze clean and forgiving
The friendly banter, tension leaving

The smooth arc of the bat, the foot stomping
The bag, the thump of the ball in the mitt,

The thumb flying up, the wave of dissension
From the throng billows on the wind,
Like the flags and bits of whirling paper,

Now cups float down, caught in the upslope
And a short, drunk Neanderthal, the kind I like,
Leaps the fence with a crazed grin and
Heads across the infield with several ushers

In pursuit, orange vests flapping like a clown's.
He makes it to centerfield, stops and shyly shakes
the baffled all-star's hand before he's swamped
by the Barnum and Bailey bleacher patrol.

The crowd cheers his audacity, but wait.
A lone figure emerges from the dugout and gestures
To the bullpen. He takes the ball from the man on the
mound, mouth full of spit, and pats his butt as he
ambles off, defeated but already planning his revenge.

The troops gather round to watch the new arm
Warm up, return to their posts, the crowd waits
The slow windup, the smooth, spinning delivery,

The clean arc of the bat, the foot stomping the bag
The thump of the ball in the mitt, the sky so clear,

The breeze forgiving, the friendly banter, the tension
Leaving.

The Blind Singer

I am the blind singer
Hurling love songs
At the silent, starving moon

The old woman
Deserted by her children,
The lost and lonely immigrant
Far from family

The force of emotion
That drives the soul into
A rushing swell of madness

This is love, what passes for it,
This is the malavit'
The raw life, the inner eye
Twisted and torn out

Thrown into the midnight sky
Doomed to look forever
At the timeless turning
At the beauties that paralyze

The hope that fails
The faith that saves
the misguided map of the heart

the aching limb lifting self
Into the only thing that matters

Now

I am the blind singer
Whose lips never falter

Whose lips never falter
Once they begin to sing.

Notes

Three quarters of the first chapter, Fatto, was written in the Last few years. Like everything in this book, they are as true as I can make them, though some are a rangia of several tales, mine and others. Memory is a funny friend. I admit to self-absorption and I've noticed a proclivity toward memorials for poets passed on. I've asked myself if I'm feeding off their history and the answer is probably, yes. Will I continue to write about them? Probably, yes.

Pg. 5 - il sangue miei morti- from Ungaretti
Pg. 9 - sapore del pianto- from Sinisgalli

Ascending blindly - An old Taoist quote, I think. I'm a font of incomplete knowledge. From the mid-90's to present.

Pg. 92 -wrote this while watching a great film of Jack reading all Ovah the Medium D, at Jimi(Og) Bernath's house with Jon (Grog) Munson. They began Denver Poets' Day in 1976 and are stalwarts since the 70's.

Survivors - I think this is called "spiritual" poetry. From mid 90's to mid 2000's. An apology for apocalyptic fever. With a dose of mad to finish. You may hate this excursion into self-inquiry existing in its own mysterious, little world. Some was rocketed on a ship to Mars.

.44 - late 80's, early 90's. as I approached my 44th birthday in '95, I felt I was staring right down a barrel. Still do! Lotsa love poems. Hmmm...

Young Horses - A smattering of oldies from the '80's. You shoulda seen the '70's. Left the crazy stuff out.

Pg. 160 -Jimmy Morris (d. 1979) was the originator of modern Denver poetry. He wrote, published and lived a parallel outsider line to another original, dynamo printer/publisher Alan Swallow, who created Denver University's Creative Writing Program. They were working on the first issue of Mile High Underground mag when Swallow died in 1966.

Ed Ward is Denver's finest storyteller as well as a poet and painter. Since the 70's, he has been the godfather, a fiery supporter of individual expression, always ready to help and inform. Marcia Ward, Ed's wife, shares the same virtues as well as being one of the Mile High City's finest photographers.

I would be remiss in not mentioning a small group of at Least fifty "heroes", those from Denver or who've passed Through and had a major influence on me. And as a host And participant in readings I've always been shocked at the wide variety of people who've blown me away, from 14 year old youngsters to old grandmas, people in rags and in suits. What a trip. I never forget. Thank you all

And to visionary poet Charlie Mehrhoff for Rocco and Blaga, to Dana Pattillo for Juan Ramon, to Tom Ferril for leading the way, to John Fante for North Denver.

Made in the USA
San Bernardino, CA
18 September 2015